Carole Killalea
721 N. Madison
Hinsdale, Ill.

One Man's Montana

An Informal Portrait of a State

One Man's

MONTANA

An Informal Portrait
of a State

By John K. Hutchens

J. B. LIPPINCOTT COMPANY
Philadelphia & New York

To the memory of my father

Contents

I *Arrival* 13

II *A Place* 17

III *The Night They Hanged the Sheriff* 23

IV *More About a Gold Camp* 33

V *Wife to the Major* 46

VI *Tommy Cruse Has His Day* 51

VII *June Sunday, 1876* 60

VIII *Great Indian* 70

IX *Just the Same, a Lady* 80

X *More Than One Way to Journey's End* 85

XI *Adolescent Interludes* 92

XII *Titans* 106

XIII *My Father's Town* 123

XIV *Exit Old West, Not Laughing* 132

XV *Mr. McGraw's Lieutenant* 138

XVI *City Room* 142

XVII *Warriors* 156

XVIII *Blood on the Bridge* 167

XIX *The Sinister City* 172

XX *Ghost Town* 178

XXI *Heroes' Reward* 185

XXII *Mr. Callahan* 193

XXIII *Charlie Russell* 201

XXIV *Return* 212

A Note

ONCE UPON A TIME *there was a book reviewer who often wrote somewhat derisively of memoirists purporting to recall, verbatim, conversations they had overheard or taken part in a good many years before. Had they, the reviewer inquired, used tape recorders in that pre-tape-recorder era? I now solemnly apologize for having failed to recognize that the form in which one sets down the truth, as in all honesty one recalls it, can be irrelevant—that it is the substance of the truth that matters. Here, then, is that substance as it appears, or rather reappears, to me, after so long.*

One Man's Montana

An Informal Portrait of a State

Arrival

I FIRST SAW IT EARLY IN THE EVENING of that July day in 1917, the vast landscape into which the westbound train rolled as it finished with North Dakota and went on toward the sunset. Montana.

It was both new and wonderful, and yet it was not really new to me. Since I could remember anything at all in my eleven—about to be twelve—years, I had been hearing of this far-off empire. My father had once lived here. My father, a young man then, had arrived in this remote land in 1889, and remained until, like other western States, Montana fell victim to the Panic of 1893, and young men like Martin Hutchens departed reluctantly to make their way elsewhere. Montana had lived on, though, in Martin Hutchens' memory as the place it was when, a newcomer from New York State and a fledgling newspaperman in Montana's capital city, Helena, he knew and cherished the pioneers who had made it a Territory and a State like no other—gold and silver miners who struck it rich or not at all, copper kings, soldiers, gamblers, gun fighters, politicians, merchants, cattlemen—all that splendid, romantic company about whom he had told stories so often and so vividly to me, the boy now gazing out of a window of the Northern Pacific's *North Coast Limited*.

It did not occur to me that Montana would or could be other than as I had imagined it.

Well, yes, even one so innocent as myself could guess that certain changes must have taken place since my father's time. This or that early-day hero would have died. Stagecoaches had given way to automobiles. Indians now lived on reservations. The old cattleman's open range was gone.

But might there not be men still living who had heard the quiet, deadly courteous voice of Henry Plummer, the sheriff-bandit, in the bars and streets of Bannack and Alder Gulch and perhaps even seen him hanged one snowy January night in 1864? Men who had known George Armstrong Custer before he set out for his fatal Sunday afternoon at the Little Big Horn? Who had watched the great Nez Percé, Chief Joseph, come through Lolo Pass from Idaho and march down the Bitter Root Valley on his 1800-mile running fight with the United States Army? Who had bet on the thoroughbred horses of Marcus Daly, the warm, shrewd, Irish copper magnate who did so much to transform little Butte into a symbol of wealth at once roistering and sinister?

If I were lucky, I thought, there might indeed be men still living who would remember such times and events, such heroes and villains.

I was lucky. There were such men. Presently I was to know some of them, nor did my luck end there. The town, and the State, in which I was to live for the next ten years were closer to my father's time than I could have dared to hope. To the west, the Pacific Coast States were long since settled, populous, orderly. To the east were the Dakotas, agrarian and flat. But Montana, as in later years I would come to realize, was then somewhere between the old frontier and modern life as other States knew it. Montana could be on civil terms with the present. More often and more typically, it seemed to be listening over its shoulder, with affectionate pride, to the voice of its violent past.

It would be a considerable while before I came to have a sense of Montana outside that part of it with which I first became acquainted: the town of Missoula, just west of the Continental Divide, where the Bitter Root River flows north into the Clark Fork of the Columbia River, 3300 feet above sea level, on a flat-floored valley ringed by the Rocky Mountains, the Sapphire range to the east, and the Missions to the north.

Of the State across which the *North Coast Limited* wove through that night and the next morning, of its size and its face, its tone and its history, I would learn in a good way: slowly and by experience. I may have known then, but hazily, that in its western area it was mountainous, in its central and eastern areas hilly and running to plains and then to badlands; that the Missouri River formed at a place called Three Forks, because three rivers came together there to become the single one that runs north and then east and southeast until it joins the Mississippi far away. I may also have been aware then, but perhaps it was later, that the first white men to travel through most of this wilderness were Lewis and Clark and their company, and after them the men who liked to travel alone, like Jim Bridger and other early scouts and trappers—the mountain men. I certainly knew that other white men flocked here, in an endlessly gaudy, fascinating pageant, almost as soon as gold was first seen to flash in the streams of Southwestern Montana.

The Indians, of course, had been here forever.

The *North Coast Limited* roared through Hell Gate Canyon, the echoes of its whistle wailing. It pulled into the Northern Pacific depot. My mother and my sister Helena (named for the city where my father had lived and been so happy in 1889-1893) and I stepped down to the platform. My father, who had preceded us from Chicago to be editor and publisher of the two local daily newspapers, the *Missoulian* (morning) and the *Sentinel* (evening), was awaiting us. No one in all the world, it was plain to see on that hot, dry, clear, sunny morning, could possibly have been more content than Martin

Hutchens, returned to the State where for so many years he had longed again to be.

Strangely, yet not so strangely, because of all that I had heard about it, the place already had a familiar look. The adventure had begun.

A Place

DID IT ALL REALLY HAPPEN, I have often wondered, as it appeared to me even then to be happening in that decade of boyhood and adolescence? The past and present joining and concurrently existing, the old frequently seeming as actual and tangible as the new?

I believe that it did happen in just that way, for in Missoula the old—as "old" went in a land that still bore the frontier's stamp—was everywhere side by side with the new and constantly intermingling with it.

Through the town, flowing west out of Hell Gate Canyon, ran the river, spanned by one modern, steel-girder bridge and one red, rickety one. North of the river was that part of the town settled in the early 1860's. By 1917 it was the business district, with separate buildings known as "blocks," and with tree-lined streets of brick and frame houses. At the north end of the main thoroughfare, Higgins Avenue, named for a co-founder of the town, stood the already grimy Northern Pacific depot and its bustling yards. Running parallel to that river, and still touched with an air of sin and excitement, were West Front Street and what remained of the old red light district, furtively alive if no longer formally licensed.

South of the river was the newer, more recently settled Missoula, where the better-off citizens lived, save for those old-timers who chose to stay on in their comfortable North

Side homes. Solid mansions lined Gerald Avenue, the homes of leading bankers, and a millionaire lumberman's widow, and a few of the lawyers who managed to make more than a grubby living around the courthouse. On streets that intersected Gerald Avenue were smaller, neatly tended homes of later-comers and older residents of more modest income. At the far end of University Avenue, under the lee of Mount Sentinel, wandered the University of Montana campus, in 1917 less than thirty years old but its red brick buildings already weather-beaten. Off to the south and west ran the prairie, where the tumble-weed rolled in the hot summer winds and the Flathead Indians came every spring to make camp and dig for tasty camas roots. Over near the Bitter Root River was Fort Missoula, erected in a hurry in the mid-1870's against the threat of an Indian attack that never came. Its original log buildings were still there, to which mission-style barracks were later added, and a regiment remained stationed on the post if only because there was nowhere else to put it in peacetime.

Was it not all—North Side, South Side, river, prairie, encircling mountains—a world set apart in its own wonder and mystery? It was. Perhaps a child lately from the crowded Midwest could sense this with a special clarity. The air smelled sweetly of pine. On the warmest day, sweat dried quickly in the clear, high air. The day ran long into the late, splendid sunset; at nine o'clock of a summer evening a boy could read a book under the open sky. The nights were unfailingly cool.

Everything about this town seemed large, perhaps because every street had mountains or prairie at its end. There was the feeling of big events, in the past or to come. Nature, huge and sometimes ominous, was just outside the door. In that very first summer I became aware of this. To the northeast, in the Blackfoot Valley, a forest fire roared for a week. Flames leaping from crown to crown of the great fir trees lighted the horizon by night. By day a powder of ashes seeped down over the town. The rain fell, the fire died, but after that I would always know what the words meant when I read that a settlement or a ranch had "burned out." There was the smell of danger, and it added to the keenness, the edge, of life, then as in the spring when the snow-water rushed out of Hell Gate Canyon through a channel just east of the rickety wooden bridge and it became a matter of honor for a band of winter-pale boys to swim across, gasping and dodging the logs that bore down on them like monsters in a nightmare.

A boy learns what, and when, he is ready to learn. His teachers and his classrooms, many of them not teachers or classrooms in the ordinary sense, are beyond counting. Thus, while I do not remember the very first day I climbed the steep stairs leading up from West Main Street to the city room of the *Missoulian* and *Sentinel*, I do remember a curious feeling of pre-recognition, as of a place that would be my home.

The city room was in fact two rooms, the brownish walls smoke-stained, pasted over with old headlines and news photographs, the desks scarred by cigarette burns, the air thick with tobacco fumes and humming with the beat of typewriters, the Associated Press wire ticking in a corner cubicle. At those desks were men with whom I was later to work and from whom I would learn as much as I was capable of absorbing. First among them, his voice booming orders from an office that looked out over West Main Street, was Martin Hutchens, editor-in-chief, a big-city newspaperman in a small town, a stocky perfectionist with small patience for stupidity but with a large tolerance for human frailty.

My father was fifty-one in that summer of 1917, but in my eyes he was ageless, because he was the inexhaustible source of wisdom, of tales without end about other days and scenes. After graduation from Hamilton College in 1888, he was a reporter on the Rome (N.Y.) *Sentinel* when—on one of those days that make a crossroads in a life—he read in a New York paper that the publisher of the Helena *Independent* had come east to recruit new, young members for his staff. Martin Hutchens applied, and was accepted. A month later he arrived in Helena, on the day before Montana Territory became a State in November, 1889.

"So you see," he used to say, not altogether seriously but not jokingly either, "I am technically a pioneer."

During what he chose to call the period of his expatriation from Montana, in the East to which he returned in 1893, he served Charles A. Dana's New York *Sun*, Pulitzer's New York *World*, Hearst's New York *Journal* and Chicago *American*, John Eastman's Chicago *Journal*. As a managing editor he had been mentor to such reporters as Marquis James, Ben Hecht, Robert J. Casey. But no other place he had known, no experience he had had elsewhere, held for him the spell of the Montana to which he now was restored. Certainly no aspect of his life, not even his distinction as a New York and Chicago newspaperman, had for me the magic of his Helena days as he recalled them on summer nights when, the next day's *Missoulian* having gone to press, we strolled home across the Higgins Avenue bridge.

In this very town, as a young reporter for the Helena *Independent*, he had covered the story of the hanging of four homicidal Indians in 1890. Years later I read his story in the *Independent* files, but at the moment he told it in such starkly specific detail that I looked back with a certain chill toward the courthouse yard where the gallows had stood. As if he had lately been in their company, he summoned back little X. Beidler, hangman for the Montana Vigilantes in the early 1860's, and Wilbur Fisk Sanders, the Vigilantes' fearless prosecutor of the famous killer-bandits headed by Henry Plummer.

"You *knew* them?" I asked. I was aware that he knew them, but I spoke out of some reflex of pure wonder, for I was deep in the reading of Professor Thomas J. Dimsdale's *The Vigi-*

lantes of Montana, a contemporary chronicle of death by gun and rope in Bannack and Alder Gulch. My father had been among giants during the giants' later days in the more sedate city of Helena. They had told him stories he never tired of telling me. He had also known Marcus Daly and "old" Tommy Cruse, the prospector who grubstaked for twenty years until he dug into the side of a hill along Silver Gulch one day. . . .

Yes, I truly was put to it, as often as not, to be sure what era I actually lived in. And as if time were not already, for me, happily askew, there were the old, old men who talked the afternoons away on hot summer lawns around the town. A boy sitting in the tree shade, on the edge of their reminiscence, could listen, and marvel, and go on listening.

These were the ancients. They were of the dawn of time. Here, in the flesh, talking, smoking, laughing, occasionally sputtering in disagreement over points of fact, were such giants as I had envisioned. Some of them had fought at Shiloh, Antietam, Gettysburg. They had crossed the plains by covered wagon and stagecoach. One had been a trooper with Reno at the Battle of the Little Big Horn, and later with Gibbon at the Battle of the Big Hole where Chief Joseph and his Nez Percé fought with a gallantry their white foes admired. One or another of my ancients had seen the last of the mountain men, had watched the open range come and go and the railroads arrive, bringing the "honyockers," or homesteaders. They, and the memories *they* inherited, were Montana's early story, or enough of it to hold me entranced.

If I listened carefully and remembered well, some flash of intuition suggested, the sum of it all could somehow be my own. So, in my mind, the portrait of a Territory and a State took form, little by little. As I later came to see, the portrait tended to be personal. It was colored by my feelings about this or that person, place or legend. But the real painters were the talkers and the people they talked about. In time the storytellers would include certain veterans in the *Missoulian* office, and courthouse politicians, retired gun fighters, a deputy sheriff so brave he didn't have to kill, and some old-time prize-ring craftsmen.

To what I heard I would later add what I read, and what I saw and experienced for myself. The portrait would not be complete—no one's portrait of Montana could be complete—but it would retain something of what Montana had meant and still means to one who first knew it almost half a century ago.

First of all, there were the old men taking their ease in comfortable chairs on the lawns throughout those long summer afternoons.

III

The Night They Hanged the Sheriff

SOMETIMES THEY WOULD TALK OFF A RIBALD TALE of Calamity Jane Cannary—and here they would look a little warily at a twelve-year-old on the edge of their circle—or they would evoke with respect the shade of Chief Joseph and his desperate march toward Canada and freedom. But when they spoke of Henry Plummer, it was with such concentration that they moved entirely into the past, leaving behind them our town and our time and the boy who was following their every word.

As if it were yesterday—it had been over fifty years before—they remembered him, and he still puzzled them. They ran on by the hour about him, and then you could see Henry Plummer rising before them once more as he walked the streets of Bannack and, later, the little towns that made up the placer mining camp of Alder Gulch, seventy-five miles away.

He was a demon. He was a fiend. They all knew that. None of them but thought he was justly hanged that Sunday night in January, 1864, on Bannack's bleak and snowy hillside. And yet . . . an ordinary bad man, a killer, is like any other, the old men would say. Such lives went out in a twanging of vigilante rope, and only the historians thought of them again.

Henry Plummer, though, was different. You could have seen it for yourself on the day he came to Bannack, then in

Idaho Territory, late in '62, a man in his late twenties, about five feet ten, lithe and good looking, with his narrow, pale face, his neat moustache, and chestnut-brown hair; his soft voice that seldom rose even in anger; his small, almost delicate hands and feet; his gallant bow for the ladies; his intelligent talk about a variety of matters: the war, and books, and the future of this great land in which they were all to prosper together. . . . He was from Connecticut or perhaps Maine, said some; from England, said others; clearly, in any case, a gentleman.

You did notice one curious thing: his eyes had no expression, none whatever. Cold, gray, they seemed to look right through you as he spoke. But then he would smile, with his mouth, and go on talking, and you would forget about that glassy stare.

To be sure, you heard—even then—a few things, but nothing that mattered greatly. A little trouble in California (about a woman); some more at Oro Fino and Florence, west of the mountains. He had killed. He said so himself. Always, of course, he had killed in self-defense. Had not many another honest man done the same thing? Beyond that, there was nothing much, nor did you ask. "West of the Red River, no questions"—so ran the old rule out here.

So he came into Bannack about Christmas time that year, with one Jack Cleveland. Reminiscing, the old men in my town noted that arrival carefully. Cleveland and Plummer riding in from the north, the one a loud-mouthed drunkard, the other very quiet, a gentleman. The one seemed to belong, the other did not, to the mining camp that was like a hundred other mining camps: a line of tents and cabins along either side of a single street in the low, barren hills, the water from Grasshopper Creek sloshing through the sluices by day and the whiskey pouring and the oaths and laughter crackling by night, and every man dreaming of the time he would make his strike and get away from there. An odd combination, those two: the black-bearded "rough" and the gentleman in neatly pressed clothes foxed with buckskin, sitting his horse gracefully. At the time, it did not seem so odd. Traveling through dangerous country, you chose such companionship as you could find. They—Plummer and Cleveland—were lately from the Sun River country, near Fort Benton at the navigable headwaters of the Missouri. There they had visited the farm the Government ran for the Blackfoot Indians, and Plummer had intended taking a boat down the Missouri to the States.

But then, as he amiably told the Bannack friends he quickly made, something quite extraordinary had happened to him. He had fallen in love. Her name was Electa Bryan, the sister of Mrs. Vail, wife of the director of the Government farm. Plummer had not, himself, been the very soul of virtue, he went on to say winningly, but now life had new meaning for him. He would make his fortune in the mines. He would marry Electa, and together they would later go East to a quiet, happy life.

Did he mean it? Did he honestly think he could do it?

The old men, mulling it over almost sixty years later, had an idea that he did. He drank a little, gambled a little. That was no crime in Bannack. He built the cabin where he and Electa would live when they were married the next year. Leading citizens sought his opinion on mining problems, and his agreeable presence in their respectable homes. He was a favorite in their polite society, and why not? A man who could quote the classics, out-waltz any male in the camp, flatter the ladies with perfect propriety—such a one was clearly an asset to the community. And when "the boys" gathered at Goodrich's saloon, he was at home there, too.

Some of the regulars at Goodrich's had known him "west of the mountains," but not much was said about that. And when one of them did refer to it even vaguely, you would see Henry Plummer's eyes go colder and grayer, and whoever was hinting at what Plummer had done in the past—well, that person shut up. One did not carelessly annoy a man reputedly able to draw and fire five times in three seconds.

Now it was February, '63, and one day a strange thing happened. In Goodrich's sat Plummer and an acquaintance named Perkins, when Jack Cleveland—the roughneck who had come to Bannack with Plummer—entered, gun in hand. Anybody could see he was looking for trouble.

"I'm chief here!" Cleveland yelled, and to Perkins: "Why don't you pay me the money you owe me?"

"I did pay it," said Perkins.

"All right," said Cleveland, but he kept toying with the gun. Then he looked at Henry Plummer and he said, sneering, "I'm not afraid of anybody."

In the next split second Bannack saw Henry Plummer in violent action for the first time. He was out of his chair in a blur of speed. He said quickly, evenly, "I'm tired of this." He fired five times and Cleveland dropped, riddled but, curiously, not quite dead.

If Cleveland had died at once, the old men used to say, the history of Montana might have been different. But he lived three hours in the cabin of Hank Crawford, who unluckily became a marked man in Henry Plummer's eyes. For what might the dying Cleveland have revealed about Plummer and the wild days west of the mountains? Plummer kept asking Crawford about that, and each time Crawford said, "Nothing." But Plummer could not believe it, and there began a stalking game, Plummer trying to lure him into a fight, Crawford somehow escaping the trap. Now the whole camp was watching and making bets on which man would kill the other. There came a day when Plummer, with a rifle, was prowling the street in search of his enemy, and Crawford, also with a rifle, saw him first. Crawford's rifle bullet went in at Plummer's right elbow, lodging in the wrist.

"Some son of a bitch has shot me," said Plummer, and walked away, and challenged Crawford to a duel two weeks hence. But Hank Crawford did not wait. He left that day for Fort Benton, the East, and safety.

Now this would have been a run-of-the-camp feud, the old men used to say, except that about then a shadow seemed to cross the winter sun of Bannack. No man's life was safe if he passed the outskirts of town. His money, if he had any, was all but certain to be taken, along with his life. The murder rate stepped up even beyond the average in gold rush camps. Was there a gang, an organization? A rumor, at first; a suspicion, no more. What a man suspected he did not say aloud, if he really wanted to go on living. Still, the shadow had not yet reached Henry Plummer. Men in Bannack did not like all the company he kept, but most of them liked Henry Plummer, the well-spoken, the courtly. In May they helped elect him sheriff. His right arm, ploughed by the bullet from Hank Crawford's rifle, had healed. While it was healing, he learned to shoot almost as skillfully with his left hand. Shortly after his election, he left for the Sun River country to marry Electa Bryan; which he did, on a June day in 1863.

They made a fine picture coming into town, the old men recalled: Electa, slight, blonde and lovely in a plain brown dress, her husband in a dark business suit, checked shirt and neat tie, and she holding his arm as they arrived in a wagon behind four Indian ponies. Now, said Henry Plummer, you would see a real sheriff. He and Electa moved into the cabin he had built, and presently the Vails came down from Sun River, bringing another friend Plummer had made there, Francis Thompson, a storekeeper. They all boarded together, and Bannack reckoned there was not a happier couple in the camp than the Plummers.

You didn't see him in the saloons at all now, or with the wild men he had known west of the mountains. A family man, a public official. His job was bigger than it was when he was elected to it, because while he was away in June a group of prospectors over in Alder Gulch, to the northeast, had found the richest placer field Montana was ever to know. Already ten thousand people were crowding into it.

And now the shadow that had crossed the winter sun became a nightmare in the summer noon. Remembering, the old men could hardly believe it, but there it was. Moreover, everyone came to know who the killers were. They were George Ives, Red Yeager, Ned Ray, Buck Stinson, Boone Helm, Hayes Lyons and a score of others. They killed and robbed in broad daylight, sometimes without masks. They swaggered in the bars and brothels of Alder Gulch, boasting about how they got their gold dust.

In Bannack, Sheriff Henry Plummer did nothing.

Nothing? The shadow crept toward him a little. There were mornings when his usually pallid face was weatherbeaten. Why was that, unless he had been night-riding on errands of his own? Why did he keep a fine saddle house at a ranch near Bannack but never bring it into town? Where was he really going when he went on those "prospecting trips" that always seemed to coincide with a holdup?

"You were sure and you weren't sure," one of the old men would say. "You talked with him a while, and you'd swear you never met a finer fellow. And who were you going to talk to about what you might have suspected? People talked, and they got killed."

Here it was September, and the bones of murdered men were in canyons from Alder Gulch to points well on the way south to Salt Lake. In the autumn Electa suddenly left Bannack for the East, by the Salt Lake stage. Her husband would meet her in Iowa the next year, she told Francis Thompson, Plummer's young storekeeper-friend. How much did she know about her husband's night-riding, secret life? She gave no sign. In Alder Gulch the blood kept flowing, and in Bannack Henry Plummer met each incoming stage and asked, "Were you held up?" His gray eyes were blank while he listened to the passengers' reports. The wary ones said they had no idea who the brigands were. Others, taking Plummer at face value, told him what they knew, and some of them died regretting it.

Still, he must have felt safe now, the money pouring in and no member of his gang yet caught. He could afford a gesture that may have been wryly humorous. The late fall had brought to Bannack a group of eminent citizens, among them Sidney Edgerton, the new Chief Justice of Idaho, and Colonel Wilbur Fisk Sanders, attorney, late of the Union Army. Would they and their families be Sheriff Plummer's guests at Thanksgiving dinner? They would, and they enjoyed themselves mightily while the host carved Salt Lake turkey and pleased the distinguished company with his elegant conversation.

Perhaps, said the old men, recalling this, he felt *too* safe; and this was the first of the things that used to puzzle them about Plummer during the long summer afternoons of reminiscing. For there was nothing in the character of Henry Plummer, a born planner, to suggest that he was one to take a chance.

But at this point he was about to take several chances.

On a December night in Alder Gulch a little group of men made desperate by the utter lack of law enforcement in this huge wilderness area, except the "law" enforced by the suspected Plummer, took a decisive step. A swaggering, handsome, reckless bandit, George Ives, robbed and killed an industrious, well-liked young German, Nicholas Tbolt, and left his body in the brush for the coyotes to gnaw at. The evidence was beyond doubt. This was too much even for Alder Gulch, accustomed as it was to casual murder. The amazed Ives was arrested at gun point, put in chains, and held for trial before a court consisting of the mining camp as a whole.

What no one could be sure of was the role the Plummer gang would play. They were noisily and ominously on hand.

So, firmly and guns in hand, were the aroused miners. Plummer himself, although he now and then came over from Bannack to look after his interests, was not there. Ives, apparently certain that Plummer's men if not Plummer himself would find a way to save him, sat unconcerned while the trial got under way.

That was something to see, the old men said—Colonel Sanders standing on a wagon box arguing for the execution of the killer, while a jury of twenty-four listened in the light of a fire built against the harrowing cold, Ives' drunken lawyer ranting, the jury coming back with its verdict of guilty which, put to popular vote, was acclaimed by all save Ives' friends. They yelled threats. The miners' gunlocks clicked. The threats stopped. It was a critical stage in Montana's history.

Colonel Sanders moved for immediate execution of the sentence.

"Give him time!" a friend of Ives called out.

"Ask him how much time he gave the Dutchman!" shouted little X. Beidler, who made his debut on the Montana scene with that suggestion.

So George Ives was hanged in the moonlight, and the next day the Montana Vigilantes were born, taking a stern oath and adopting as their sign the numerals 3-7-77 (the dimensions of a grave, three feet wide, seven feet long, seventy-seven inches deep). But even now Henry Plummer did not take warning, nor early the next month when a Vigilante group caught Red Yeager and George Brown and hanged them, too. Others in the gang were heading west, but the chief stayed on in Bannack.

Why?

The old men couldn't answer that one. He must have known that at least one of his highwaymen would betray him, hoping to save his own neck. One of them did. But Henry Plummer was still there on Sunday morning, January 10, 1864.

The Night They Hanged the Sheriff

Listening to the account of what happened in Bannack on that climactic day, I used to feel that I had lived through every moment of it; because two of the old men who talked about it had been there in fact, and it was not a day whose slightest detail a witness would be apt to forget throughout his life.

After a morning and afternoon of cold and silence, the winter dusk fell early. The empty street was still. In the cabin where he boarded, Plummer lay down after supper to rest, and for once—of all times—he put his .45 caliber revolver on a chair beyond his easy reach. He apparently did not hear the footsteps on the bridge that crossed the creek, or the opening of the cabin door. What he saw first was a man telling him he was wanted. For a moment, then, he faltered, but recovered and made a move toward his gun while his fellow boarders, the Vails and Francis Thompson, looked on in amazement. His visitors got to the gun first. His white face went whiter, but he said nothing and marched into the waiting group outside and on down the street to where others were standing with Buck Stinson and Ned Ray, acknowledged members of the Plummer gang.

Now this was the end, the old men said, and if it were only a matter of hanging Ray and Stinson, no one would have remembered it fifty-odd years later. But there was this third man, this Henry Plummer. There they stood, the three of them, under a gallows where Sheriff Plummer had executed a murderer only the summer before.

The wind blew icily across the snow while Stinson and Ray died quickly, screaming as they went. Plummer did not scream. It was worse, the old men said. He cried.

"Oh, God!" he moaned—and they could hear him still—"Oh, God! I'm too wicked to die!"

The recently organized Vigilantes stood around him in silence, the gale biting them, and still no one moved. They knew he had to die, but none of them could believe it even now. Ives and Yeager and the others, yes; but not Henry

Plummer. Now he was sobbing, and asking them to cut out his tongue and cut off his ears and send him into the storm, but not to hang him.

Out of the shadows a Vigilante leader said, "You can't feel harder about it than I do," and in a way it was true. And, "Bring up the rope," he said, and a boy handed the rope to a man who fixed the noose under Henry Plummer's left ear and tied his wrists behind his back.

Here it was, the last moment of one they had all talked with or had a drink with, and had liked.

"Lift him up," the Vigilante leader said.

Four men moved forward, and they lifted Henry Plummer as high as they could. Then, for a second, they waited, because this still was not quite real.

In the calm voice of the Plummer they had known, he said, "Please give me a good drop."

They dropped him, the rope twanged, the body jolted and turned slowly from side to side while they stood watching him in silence. Then they went back to the town.

Yes, the old men used to say, he was rightly hanged. But, they also said, when you saw it happen it kind of got you. You couldn't say exactly why, because he certainly deserved to die as much as others in his outfit did, and likely more so. They guessed it was because he was—well, so much like a gentleman. Then, with the late-afternoon shadows settling across the lawn, they would get to talking about what made him what he was—whether he was greedy or weak or just a natural killer—but to those questions they did not pretend to have a final answer, and I suspected they preferred it that way. Still guessing, they would be able to meet another day and hash it all over again, and so on, indefinitely.

IV

More About a Gold Camp

1.

IT WAS A HELL OF A TIME in Alder Gulch and its metropolis, Virginia City, my ancient friends used to say, because even if you struck it rich—and the odds were against this—your chances of keeping what you got, or of living to enjoy it, were not great. Just what were you going to do if Boone Helm made up his mind to rob you? Henry Plummer had, at least, the gift of finesse. Boone Helm was an animal. He would stab you in daylight and spend your gold dust that night in the saloons and brothels.

The veterans all but shuddered, remembering him: the huge, whiskey-crazy Kentuckian who killed for the fun of it and was known to have eaten two of his victims, one of them an Avenging Angel in the service of Brigham Young. He had brawled and slaughtered from Missouri to San Francisco and north to Vancouver. But then, four days after Henry Plummer died in Bannack, the string ran out even for Boone Helm, the apparently indestructible one. With Frank Parish, Clubfoot George Lane, Jack Gallagher and Hayes Lyons, he was arrested by the now confident Vigilantes. For once, he saw no way to shoot his way out of a difficult situation. Instead, he asked for a Bible and declared he was ready to swear his innocence on it. A Bible was brought to him.

33

"By God, he swore it again, kissing that Bible," said one of the old men, even now scarcely able to believe the sacrilege. It did Helm no good, though. He called for a drink of whiskey—Virginia City would not refuse that to anyone at all—and with his four fellow killers was placed on a dry-goods box under a cross-beam in an unfinished log building. He looked on with some contempt while Clubfoot George asked a local citizen to pray with him. The delay irritated Helm.

"For God's sake, if you're going to hang me, do it and get through with it," he said. "There goes one to hell," he growled when Clubfoot George jumped into space. "Every man for his principles! Hurrah for Jeff Davis! Let her rip!" he yelled when his own turn came.

Was it a brave man's nerve? A stupid man's bravado? I used to puzzle over this, nor am I yet sure.

In any case, the old men used to say, the town breathed more easily. The terror was over. There was even a good deal of rough humor, in retrospect, about the whole gory time. The man who adjusted the nooses that day was little X. Beidler, of whom a sympathetic bystander later asked a question.

"Didn't you feel for him, just a little?" The bystander named one or another of the five who were hanged.

"Yes, I did. I felt for his left ear," said little X.

The Vigilantes were almost, but not entirely, done with their work. There remained one task about which the old men, these many years later, were still uneasy. Was Joseph A. Slade justly hanged? Slade—"Slade of the Overland." I listened carefully. No less a one than Mark Twain, in a work to which I had lately become devoted, *Roughing It*, had been fascinated by him. Mark Twain had actually met him when, in the days of his glory, Slade was the highly efficient if tyrannical division boss for the Great Overland Stage, maintaining order and service over a 600-mile route plagued by Indians and horse thieves. But here were men some of whom had been present when Slade came to the end of the trail. Now I would hear the inside story, or, anyhow, an eyewitness version, a close-up. It was not to work out quite that way. Something like regret, perhaps even shared guilt, made for a certain reticence about Slade's death.

Like Henry Plummer, they said, Slade was personable and superficially courteous. Unlike Henry Plummer, he was fiercely honest. His courage and integrity moved Professor Thomas J. Dimsdale to say of him, in *The Vigilantes of Montana:* "From Fort Kearney west, he was feared a great deal more than the Almighty"—a phrase much admired by Mark, who, after quoting it in *Roughing It*, added, "For compactness, simplicity and vigor of expression, I will back that sentence against anything in literature."

What happened, then, to turn Slade of the Overland into the dangerous hell-raiser he admittedly became? What happened, said the old men, was that the United States Army prevailed on the Overland to fire Slade after he violently wrecked the sutler's quarters at an army fort along the Overland's route. Slade did not want liquor sold to his employees; it impaired their efficiency. By a sad irony, the jobless and bitter Slade then took to drinking heavily himself. He drifted into Alder Gulch, bringing his regal, black-haired, frontier-bred wife, Virginia, a remarkable horsewoman and an excellent shot.

For a while all went well with him. He was a respected merchant. Far from being of the Plummer faction, he was a Vigilante. But his drinking grew increasingly irresponsible, for reasons never quite clear, unless it was simply that he enjoyed getting drunk. He rode his horse into saloons and stores and broke up the furnishings, including (the last word in destruction in that time and place) the scales on which gold was weighed. He later paid for what he destroyed, and apologized, and then he did it all over again.

Finally, arrested once more after X. Beidler had given him

a friendly warning to go home to his ranch, he held a pistol to the judge's head and escaped punishment, but only temporarily. Only the evening before, at the local theater, he had offended respectable citizens and their wives by shouting to a dancer to remove her clothes. This time the Vigilantes meant to get rid of him, and they did, while he pleaded for a chance for a final word with his wife, twelve miles away on their ranch. The Vigilantes, knowing her temper and her way with a gun, declined. The judge at whose head he had held a gun tried to save him with a speech. It failed. Down from a gallows beam went Slade to his death, only a few minutes before his wife, summoned by a messenger of Slade's, rode up in fury. She denounced his sometime friends for having failed to shoot him down on the gallows. Better the bullet than the rope, she screamed. There was no answer.

Were they already, I used to ask myself, faintly ashamed? For, of course, I lacked the nerve to ask this of the old men who had been on the scene. None, I observed, spoke of having been a participant in the execution. Something about their cautious recollection of it suggested that they agreed with those Virginia City people who described Slade's hanging as the Vigilantes' one mistake. Whatever his misdemeanors, he had killed no one in Montana. He was not executed after a trial. He was lynched because he was a nuisance and because, sooner or later, he might have killed someone, and probably would have. But, after all, they could have solved the problem merely by banishing him as they had banished others. A romantic young listener was not happy about this. He sensed that his elders were not happy about it, either.

In a tin coffin filled with preservative alcohol, Joseph A. Slade went to Salt Lake City for burial. To Salt Lake, in due course, went the former Mrs. Slade as the wife of James Kiskadden, Virginia City merchant and friend of her late husband. Their marriage ending in a divorce, Mr. Kiskadden married Miss Annie Adams, actress. Their daughter, likewise to be an actress, was Maude Kiskadden Adams. At about the time I heard the story in which the first Mrs. Kiskadden had figured, I was taken to see Miss Maude Adams at the Liberty Theater, in Missoula, in "A Kiss For Cinderella," her last stellar vehicle before her long retirement from the stage. Sir James M. Barrie's dramatic lollipop seemed very far from the tumult of Alder Gulch where Miss Adams' father had been an actor in another kind of cast.

2.

I found all this excitement superb to ponder and imagine, and greatly regretted that I was not born in time to be a part of it. In lieu of that, I could not help meditating occasionally on what day-by-day life was like in Alder Gulch between the deeds of violence and retribution. Did people enjoy themselves there? Was it a good place to live in? I finally dared, haltingly, to put such questions to one or another of the old men.

They did not answer at once. They smiled. How much should they tell a mere boy about a camp that, when on its best behavior, was never mistaken for a missionary station? But then, as usual, they got to talking among themselves and forgot that I was there.

Oh, yes, I could see and hear it then as they went on: the gulch that ran twelve miles from Bald Mountain down to the Valley of the Pas-sam-a-ri, the Shoshone Indian word for Stinking Water, now politely called the Ruby River; the three settlements above Virginia City—Pine Grove, Highland, Summit—and the three below it, Junction, Nevada, Central. But Virginia City was the place, the center, the capital.

"God A'mighty, the noise!" one old man would say, and I could hear the shouting and the brawling, the violins in the hurdy-gurdy houses, the cracking of the bullteam freighters' whips, the gunfire that sometimes was exuberant and aimless and sometimes was calculated and sinister.

"The booze," another would say. "That made for a lot of noise." They called it "tangle-leg" and "tarantula juice," "forty-rod" and "pop-skull," and as often as not it was concocted from boiled mountain sage, plug tobacco steeped in water, and cayenne pepper. It sold for fifty cents a drink.

"The girls," said another. They spoke a bit circumspectly of the girls, but also with what I took to be an air of happy memory. Were they pretty, or did they only seem pretty to men in a place where women were rare?

"The girls in the hurdy-gurdies were pretty," a sage insisted. "Didn't have to be whores, either." The word startled me. "Not at a dollar a dance, all night long, and the girl getting half of it. Presents, too. All that gold dust on the side. A girl could get along all right."

"The ones in the cribs, not much to look at." Cribs? The term was new to me.

"Got all wore out quick."

"Not the Chink girls. Beautiful, like little dolls."

"Cost a lot."

"Worth it."

"I wouldn't have said it then, but we didn't treat the Chinks right. Hard-working little fellas. Tended to their own business."

"Tough in a fight, too, if you pushed 'em too far. They'd take a knife in one hand, hatchet in the other. I tangled with one. Lucky to get away alive."

The week's great day in Alder Gulch was Sunday, as I could tell by simply listening. The hurdy-gurdy girls, in handsome silks, riding down Wallace Street in open carriages. Fights, with fists or more serious weapons, breaking out all through the day. Horse races down on the valley floor, money changing hands from one buckskin bag to another.

"Funny thing, how some of those holy rollers took to the new life when they got away from the life back home."

"That minister from Georgia, name of Wood, wasn't he? Was taking eight hundred– a thousand a day out of his claim. Bought a barrel of whiskey for four hundred dollars—sounds like a lot of money but it wasn't, what with the freight from Salt Lake City—tied a tin cup to it, set it up like a drinking fountain for anybody wanted a drink. Got so drunk himself he sold his claim for just about nothing, had to live off his friends."

"Bill Fairweather throwing his money into the street to watch the Chinks scramble for it, and him the main discoverer of the whole thing, him and Henry Edgar. Know what old Bill said that day? He panned a good nugget first try he made. He stood there looking at the water and he yelled, 'This gold'll last till the cows come home.' "

"Died a drunk, didn't he?"

"At Robber's Roost in 'seventy-five. Where Plummer's boys hung out."

"Bummer Dan!"

"Sold his claim for a few thousand, went back to the States. Somebody took a million out of it later."

They were playing a memory game, now, with names.

"Thomas Francis Meagher!"

No one, for a moment, took up that name, the Irish patriot who was condemned to death for his role in the 1848 uprising in his native land, had his sentence commuted to exile to Tasmania, escaped to America, led the Irish Brigade in the Army of the Potomac, was appointed secretary of the Territory of Montana in 1865, became Acting Governor, and fell or was pushed to his death from a Missouri River steamboat near Fort Benton in 1867.

"I was with him at Antietam," said one old man quietly, "when we charged the Bloody Lane. There was nothing or nobody he was afraid of."

"I heard him speak the day he got to Virginia City in 'sixty-five," said another. "Never heard a man could put words together like him, old Bryan or Ingersoll or anybody else, a voice with music in it, like a bugle."

"Right now I'd kill the man who killed him, if somebody did kill him," said the man who had been with Meagher at Antietam. Then: "Those Goddamn Secesh men! Maybe it was one of them. There was more of 'em than us in Alder Gulch."

The passion of old enmity rang in his words, but then, surprisingly, he chuckled. "One of 'em tried to name Virginia City 'Varina,' after Jeff Davis' wife. Didn't get away with it."

"Con Orem!" said one of the old men, going on with the memory game.

"I'll always say he won the fight," said another.

The fight with Hugh O'Neil, he meant. It was Montana's first professional prize fight, its longest, and probably its most bitterly debated one: 185 rounds, under the London Prize Ring rules—a knockdown ended a round—on a January afternoon in 1865. A fine little gentleman, John Condel Orem, said the old men; a saloon keeper who did not drink, a Fancy Dan with his buckskin-covered hands, an Ohio boy, a true-blue American, standing five feet six and a half, weighing 138 pounds. His opponent, O'Neil, from County Antrim, was a hard-drinking freighter, two inches taller than Orem, and heavier by fifty-odd pounds. The agreement was for a thousand dollars a side, a share of the gate, and whatever money their friends might want to toss into the ring after the battle.

The battle ended after some three and a half hours when Orem had been knocked down fifty times, O'Neil falling on him and slugging him when both were down, and O'Neil on the ground eighteen times, while their partisans fought among themselves and yelled "Foul!"

"A rough piece of work it was," said one of the old men, "and damn exciting, too, and the referee was right to stop it, with O'Neil blinded in both eyes and Con so pounded he couldn't walk."

"Who won?" I asked.

"Neither one of them," said the old man. "It was a draw, and all bets off, and no more than four hundred dollars or so for each of them out of the ticket money, and a share of the gold tossed into the ring."

Without paying out so much as a pinch of gold dust, a man in Virginia City could see all the fights he wanted to watch and do all the fighting he felt up to himself, the old man went on to say. It was the town's favorite form of entertainment, especially in the winter when most of the workings along the gulch were closed down and the male population was bored and looking for excitement. Now and then a theater troupe arrived, the Chapmans or the Langrishes, but a rousing street fight held first place, or a semi-organized one on a Sunday afternoon when two miners stripped to the waist and celebrated the Sabbath by hammering each other until one of them dropped.

"The wonder was we stayed alive," said one old man contentedly. "If it wasn't a fight, fists or guns, it was the mud. A man could get drowned in it, winter or spring, and that's a fact. And the stench—I can smell it now! Ten thousand people, up and down the gulch, and the outhouses reeking the year round."

"It was the fine air kept us going," said another, "and the good spring water. There was no sickness to keep a doctor busy."

"Only one kind," said the other, looking past me, "and it was a fellow's own fault if he caught it."

Brief silence.

Because I was always imagining myself as a boy in Virginia City, I finally got around to asking what a twelve-year-old (by no coincidence, my own age) found to do there. I knew, of course, what *I* would have done there. I would have gunned down Henry Plummer when he held up the stage I was taking from Alder Gulch to Bannack. I would have trained faithfully and knocked out the tough bully-boy, Hugh O'Neil, with a single punch, thus avenging little Con Orem, slugged when he was down.

"God A'mighty, those kids in Virginia City!" said an old man, and turned to me. "You'd have had a fine time there. You'd have got a job at Mr. Kiskadden's store, no wages but all the stray gold dust you could sweep off the floor, maybe five dollars a day. You'd have thrown rocks at the Chinks, and if a Chink kid threw one back and caught you in the eye with it, it would have served you right. If your old man was a placer miner, you'd have learned to raise the colors in a pan of gravel. If he was a freighter or a mule skinner, you'd have learned to crack a whip so it sounded like there was firecrackers on the end of it. You'd have gone to Professor Dimsdale's school."

"No, sir," I said. "I wouldn't have wanted to go to school."

"Professor Dimsdale's school was different," the old man said. "Ask Mollie Sheehan."

I didn't know anybody by the name of Mollie Sheehan, I said.

"Mrs. Ronan," said the old man impatiently. "Mrs. Peter Ronan."

Then Mollie Sheehan must be the widow of Major Ronan, for many years the Government's Indian Agent on the Flathead Reservation, a noble exception among the shameless thieves who usually were appointed to those posts. She must then also be the mother of Miss Margaret Ronan, who in a year or two would be trying earnestly to instruct me in English Literature at Missoula County High School. Did the gentlemen think it would be all right if I went to see Mrs. Ronan?

"Mind your manners when you do," said one of the old men. "There was no prettier little girl in Alder Gulch than Mollie Sheehan. There's no finer lady in this State than Mrs. Ronan."

3.

What right had I, I asked myself, to be taking the time of the widow of Major Ronan? How could she help being perplexed or amused when I telephoned to ask her permission to call upon her?

But when I arrived at the little frame house she shared with her daughter, I was received with the grave courtesy that gives a child to understand that he is being regarded as an adult. There were cakes and tea. There were pictures of old Virginia City, and Indians, and mission priests who came to the wilderness before the miners did. I had intended to ask Mrs. Ronan at once about Professor Dimsdale, my literary hero, whose *The Vigilantes of Montana* was the first book published in the Territory and ever since has been required reading for Montanans of every age. Instead, envisioning myself as a contemporary of the child she had been in Virginia City, I must have asked what it was like to be a youngster there.

Old Mrs. Ronan, small and blue-eyed and with a wisp of brogue, told me what I most wanted to hear. It was wonderful to be a child there, she said.

A child—the child she was—saw things as her elders did not. It was only later that Mollie Sheehan realized that the handsome ladies riding through the streets in their finery were not all they might be, as the sniffy phrase went. At the time, they seemed only to be handsome ladies. This was quite enough for Mollie Sheehan. Jack Gallagher, the bandit who was hanged with Boone Helm and four others, was not—

43

to her—a bandit. He had been in the wagon train that brought
Mollie and her parents from Salt Lake to Bannack, and on
the long trail he had praised her when she read aloud by the
campfire at night. What could he have done that was so bad
that his life must be taken? She would have to wait to learn.
She liked the soft-spoken Jack Gallagher as she liked the
gentle Jesuit, Father Giorda, who came to Virginia City
from afar to say Mass in a cabin with a dirt floor and an altar
decorated with pine boughs, and received with thanks the
gold dust poured into a tin cup as collection. In the spring
Mollie and her friends wandered into the hills to pick butter-
cups and snow lilies, with never a thought of danger. At
dancing parties the fiddler, knees crossed, tapped one foot
and swung the other while the small guests paced their way
through the *varsovienne*. And July 4—there, now, was a
day for the young ones, riding down Wallace Street in dead-
axle wagons drawn by mules, each State represented by a little
girl carrying a sign with its name, and one girl—the prettiest
—impersonating Columbia herself. Was it perhaps Mollie
Sheehan, I asked? The former Mollie Sheehan blushed.

But about Professor Dimsdale, Mrs. Ronan said. I did want
to know about him and about his school? I had said nothing
at all about this, and could only assume that one of my
ancient friends had been in touch with her and waggishly
quoted me as saying that no school could be much fun, not
even a school conducted by the author of *The Vigilantes of
Montana*.

A dear, quiet little Englishman was Thomas Josiah Dimsdale, said Mrs. Ronan tenderly. A learned one, too. Had I not
observed that many of its chapters were headed by classical
quotations? I had—and some of them were properly bloody,
too. (Chapter V: "Will all great Neptune's Ocean wash this
blood clean from my hand?"—*Macbeth*.) A North of England man, he had been intended for the church, by way of
Rugby and Oxford. Family financial problems sent him in-

stead to Canada, and the rigors of Ontario's climate sent him in turn to the high, dry Rockies of Montana. Probably tuberculosis already was in him, but between the Professor's arrival in Virginia City in 1863 and his death three years later he was steadily busy. His school, at two dollars a pupil, a week, flourished. He edited Montana's first newspaper of consequence, the *Montana Post*, for which he wrote editorials in the grand manner. He served as a lay reader for Virginia City's Episcopalians. He wrote his book.

He was writing it, Mollie Sheehan later suspected, during classes in his schoolroom near the base of Boot Hill where numerous of the book's principals were buried. He looked up occasionally from his writing, she remembered, smiled pleasantly and vaguely, and returned to his own work. His pupils loved him. He knew everything, and spared the rod, even when he discovered that they had slipped out of the room for mid-morning excursions into Daylight Gulch as he wrote on and on.

As if the pleasure had been all hers, old Mrs. Ronan thanked her young visitor for coming to see her and asked if he would care to hear some day about Major Ronan and his Flathead Indians. Some of the older ones, she noted casually, had seen Lewis and Clark when they came through Western Montana in 1805.

Was it not odd, she asked, about time and the way it passes? Like a clock that, as often as not, runs backwards.

I had suspected this for some time and by now was all but sure of it.

Wife to the Major

THERE WAS OLD MRS. RONAN, serving tea and cakes again and giving not the slightest hint of surprise that a young visitor had taken her at her word and come back to hear of what later happened to a little girl named Mollie Sheehan who had lived in the gold camp known as Alder Gulch. What happened to little Mollie Sheehan, she said, was that she had the great good fortune to marry a splendid man named Peter Ronan, who for sixteen years beginning in 1877 served with unfailing honesty and devotion as Superintendent of the Flathead Indian Reservation. Oh, yes, said the former Mollie Sheehan, as a girl in Helena, after her days in Virginia City, she had had a fine time, and then she had moved to California with her parents. To California in 1873 came Peter Ronan, some fifteen years older than herself, whom she had known—but she was a child then and he was an adult—when he was a newspaper editor in Virginia City and Helena. Now, when he came to California to marry her, she was twenty-one, of an age for the new life opening out before her.

"Thank goodness," said old Mrs. Ronan.

Back went the bride and groom to Helena, where Peter Ronan had one more go at journalism. Then, weary of seeing his newspaper offices burned out, he turned briefly to mining, and to a term as deputy sheriff in Helena, before he was appointed to the Flathead Reservation post. Somehow—he never took it quite seriously—this brought with it the courtesy title of Major. The man and the position, it was immediately apparent, were made for each other.

It was a happy life, Mrs. Ronan was telling me now, if not an altogether easy one for a man like Major Ronan, who believed in working at his job. For one thing, although it was called the Flathead Reservation, its population included not only Flatheads but Shoshones, Blackfeet and Nez Percés. They did not always get along well with one another. It did make things easier for the Major, an Irishman and a Catholic, that he had an agreeable relationship with the Jesuits, who since 1854 had been conducting the St. Ignatius Mission, twenty miles or so from the site of Major Ronan's Indian Agency headquarters, in a broad, fertile valley under the lee of the Western Montana Rockies.

They were great men, those pioneer priests, Mrs. Ronan said affectionately, the first of them a team consisting of a Hollander, Father Adrien Hoecken, and a Swiss, Father John Menetrey. Elsewhere in Montana, when they arrived, bitter Indian battles were ahead, General George Armstrong Custer's with the Sioux and Cheyennes and Nez Percé Chief Joseph's with the United States Army. But at St. Ignatius Mission, when Major Ronan came to the Reservation, there had been peace for more than twenty years.

How, I wondered, had those early priests managed to get along so well with their charges, at least some of whom regarded the white man's religion—the chanting and the prayers —simply as another kind of magic to be valued for its aid in stealing the horses of neighboring tribes? Mrs. Ronan chided me only gently. A good priest, she said, dealt with an Indian as the human being he was and did not insist upon too much too soon. At the first Easter service at St. Ignatius in 1855, a thousand Indians came to chant and pray in their own languages. Indian women received Communion with papooses strapped to their backs. An Indian making his confession did not have to do so verbally; he placed sticks of different lengths and sizes on the floor, representing the relative gravity of his sins. And there were jokes, said Mrs. Ronan, smiling at the memory of them. A Father Bandini, an excitable little Italian, was about to enter the confessional when he ran head-on into a black bear emerging from it. Indian witnesses to this curious encounter turned away with what sounded like a Flathead chuckle.

She didn't want to seem critical of Protestant workers in the vineyard, said Mrs. Ronan—everybody loved a Methodist circuit rider called Brother Van—but what denomination other than the True Faith would have sent four ladies from Montreal by way of the Isthmus of Panama, San Francisco and Vancouver to open a school in Western Montana? They were Sisters of Charity of Providence, and they enjoyed every minute of their journey, including the honor of being the first white women to ride across the Coeur d'Alene Mountains, an adventure they had been told no white woman could endure. Arriving at last, they astounded the natives by their enthusiasm for manual labor. They cleaned, scrubbed, swept. They instructed the Indian girls in baking, the boys in gardening, and both in music. The Federal Government's contribution to its young Indian wards being all of eight dollars a pupil a year, the four nuns and a priest went on a fund-raising tour of Montana's rough-and-tumble gold camps. "They didn't believe how much gold dust they'd bring back from Alder Gulch, but I could have told them," said the former Mollie Sheehan, who after all had lived there. "Gold dust, and the prayers of men who hadn't prayed in a long time. Four nuns on Wallace Street, a year after Boone Helm was hanged there!"

They liked and respected one another, the mission fathers and the new Superintendent, who could not have been more unlike his recent and venal predecessors—notable and typical among them the Superintendent who, when appealed to by

48

the Indians for warm clothing, sent two bolts of muslin and entered it in his official report as an expenditure of a thousand dollars.

"I wish some of those Alder Gulch miners could have had a little talk with that man," said the gentle Mrs. Ronan.

For the Ronans at the Indian Agency headquarters the years rolled happily along, no doubt because there were more and more Ronans, eight children in all. Impressive dignitaries from Washington, then as now given to all-expenses-paid junkets to far places, were frequent visitors and inevitably were charmed by the Major's anecdotal gift. An honest Indian Agent!—it was hardly to be believed. Still, all the way to the day he died in 1893 the Major was seldom without his problems, some of them grim. There was, for instance, the case of the four Indians arrested for murder in 1890 by Sheriff Bill Houston of Missoula.

None of them was a Flathead, but they lived on the Flathead Reservation and thus belonged to the Major's community. There was no question of their guilt, and the Major could not try to save them. He could only grieve and promise that their own tribes, the Pend d'Oreilles and the Kootenais, would bury them on the Reservation.

"They were only children!" old Mrs. Ronan exclaimed. She was not sentimental about the Indians, she insisted; but almost always such killing as this was brought on by whiskey, and who but the white man introduced the Indian to that?

There came the day for the hanging of the four Indians—December 19, 1890, in Missoula—on which Mrs. Ronan, this long time after, chose not to dwell, obviously because it was too painful to recall. Her husband was there, as he probably had to be in his official capacity. Present also, as I knew because I had heard him talk about it, was a young staff writer for the Helena *Independent*, Martin Hutchens. At the end of the day, riding back to Helena in the baggage car of a Northern Pacific train, his notes spread across two or three trunks, he wrote a long story that—as I realized in later years when I could appreciate it—was in the great tradition of descriptive newspaper reporting. It was the best writing he ever did, he once told me, but that was long after my conversation with Mrs. Ronan.

"What was it really like, that day?" I asked him when I came home from my visit with her.

"Some day I'll tell you" he said, "or I'll dig up the story I wrote. I can tell you now what I could never forget, the last second just before the trap was sprung. One of the four Indians on the gallows cried out 'Good-bye, Major,' but the Major didn't answer. He tried to, but he couldn't, because his eyes were full of tears and his throat was twitching. . . . I must call on Mrs. Ronan myself, one of these days," my father added. "We would have a lot to talk about."

VI

Tommy Cruse Has His Day

HAD MRS. RONAN, my ancient friends asked me, told me everything I wanted to know? Not everything, I said, but a good deal, and she had promised to tell me more. Good, they said, and went on talking about him—about old Tommy Cruse, who apparently seemed old even when he was young. Old Tommy finally showed 'em, didn't he? Yes, he did.

Tommy Cruse, from County Cavan, Ireland. The name rang familiarly, doubtless because my father had mentioned him now and again. There was no one in all Montana like Tommy Cruse, said my father, who had passed many an hour with him in Helena in the early 1890's. Tommy, the lone prospector, long unsuccessful; *Mister* Cruse, after his great day on a hillside up north of Helena, on Silver Creek; *Colonel* Cruse, when he achieved a magnate's eminence.

But the first to know him included these pioneers who had met him on the hard, bitter way along the trail, worked the same placer streams with him, dug for gold in camps long since crumbled into dust and bat-ridden shadows. One man had heard this about him, another one that. As they talked the afternoon away, I too thought I could see him, the Irishman who landed in New York in 1856 at twenty, toiled there at the grinding jobs the New World offered an Irish immigrant, headed West in 1863, prospected in the California and Nevada fields for two years, and arrived in Alder Gulch in 1865.

51

He was too late. He had always been too late. Maybe the Salmon River mines over in Idaho would be better? They were not. Then, in 1867, he came to Helena, that flourishing yet (as western towns went) oddly sedate settlement that rambles up the eastern slope of the Continental Divide and from there looks out across the wide, flat floor of the Valley of the Prickly Pear. There was still gold in Helena's Last Chance Gulch. A man digging the foundation for a store or a house was apt to find enough gold to pay for the building of it, Tommy Cruse heard. But none of that gold was for Tommy Cruse.

He was thirty-one now, but he looked older, a weather-beaten, silent man. Friendly folk in that well-mannered, charming town gave him their sympathy and now and then a grubstake for supplies when in spring the country opened and he set out on the old, heartbreaking search. Among them were not the local bankers, who laughed noisily when he called on them one day for a loan. And there were those who simply smiled when they passed him on the street. Clearly the "old man" was by now a little crazy? Frequently they said so, too loudly, and the green, Celtic eyes of Tommy Cruse were seen to darken.

So it went, spring after spring, for nine years after his arrival in Helena. Now, in April, 1876, he was on his lonely way again, placer mining day by day along a creek twenty-two miles north of the town where he had holed up disconsolately through another long Montana winter. In the bed of Silver Creek the gold quartz "float" was smooth and average. Soon it was rougher and more than average. Then, definitely, there was none at all.

Old Tommy's blood must have been racing hard as a certain possibility flashed across his miner's mind. Float quartz comes usually, if not always, from a mother lode from which it has weathered away and traveled. The rougher it is, the closer it must be to its starting point.

Tommy Cruse Has His Day

Maybe this time? He left the stream and moved up through the timber. He dug in. And there, suddenly, it was: the vein, a foot wide, of gold-shot rock, gold at the grass roots, the prospector's old, glorious dream.

Did this one yell it out, the dour, seldom-speaking man—"Gold at the grass roots!"—in the stillness of that April day? I have always wanted to believe so. Still, the years of failure had taught him caution. He staked his claim, then sat guarding his shallow discovery shaft through the afternoon. When night fell he hurried across country to Helena to register his claim in the morning.

At last, surely, he was safe? Not yet. Secretly and alone, he attacked the discovery shaft. Water seeping into it drove him out. He covered the shaft with brush, and at a point lower on the hill went to work on a tunnel that would drain the water and tap the vein somewhere on its way to the dazzling outcropping he had chanced on. For six months he sweated at it, a foot a day through solid rock, a hole barely large enough for one man to crawl in. The stories stray travelers took back to Helena said what Helena had long suspected The old man must really be crazy.

Half a year, two hundred feet to the vein. And there it was, the mother lode, the bonanza. This was it. Now he had it. The Drum Lummon, he would call it, after his native parish in Ireland. By any name at all, Montana's greatest gold quartz mine, then or ever.

It was now that he became *Mister* Cruse, and no more patronizing smiles on the streets of Helena. Was Mr. Cruse interested in selling his Drum Lummon? Mr. Cruse was not, at least for the present. Mr. Cruse was busy developing his marvelous property. By 1880 he had extracted one million dollars from it. By 1882 he was ready, but not overeager, to consider offers. They came in plenty, and the one he finally accepted was that of an English syndicate on terms giving him one and one-half million dollars in cash and stock guaranteeing him one-third of the syndicate's future profits—which, first to last, were to be some fifteen million dollars.

Long ago and far away, now, the squalid mining camps of his early years, the cheap whiskey, the beans and hard tack, the pick that rose and fell hour after hour and hit only barren rock. Now it was "Good morning, Mr. Cruse," and "Mr. Cruse, is it your opinion, sir, that. . . ?"

In his triumph he was neither more nor less friendly than before. He was himself, silent and cautious. If Nate Vestal chose to sell his Penobscot mine for half a million, blow the money on high living back East, and come home a year later to work for three fifty a day in the mine that once was his—well, that was Nate's business. Tommy Cruse had a better idea. What safer way to keep his money than to build his own bank and keep his own money in his own vault? So, in 1887, there was the Thomas Cruse Savings Bank, a neat brick building in Last Chance Gulch, with a shrewd local politician, Thomas H. Carter, to act as his adviser in the technical details of banking law.

And perhaps, too, the time had come for a newly risen magnate to take his place in society, to insure the carrying on of his line and his fortune?

The old men chatting on the lawns in my town were not exactly cynical about it, but they did allow that under the circumstances it was not altogether remarkable that Mr. Cruse found a wife with no great difficulty—no less a one than the sister of Mr. Carter.

There was a day for you, the old men used to recall, that wedding day of Mr. Cruse and Miss Margaret Carter. He never had been one for ostentation, and he never would be again; but, after all, this was an occasion like no other in his life.

"Sixteen hundred quarts of champagne came all the way from Chicago," one pioneer would remember. Now, in the hot summer sun he seemed almost to taste it again.

Tommy Cruse Has His Day

"They kept the water coolers in the Cosmopolitan Hotel filled with champagne all day," another would say, with a lingering amazement.

"From sunup to midnight, every drink in town was on Tommy, whatever saloon you went to."

"They came on horseback from a hundred miles around."

"Tommy in that Prince Albert coat, and those white gloves and tie."

"Him and his lady riding off in that platform wagon to the old Northern Pacific station after the banquet, and the crowds still so big in the saloons you couldn't get near the bar. I saw the bottles broken at the neck and passed back into the crowd and thrown empty into the street."

"That day cost him thirty thousand if it cost him a cent."

When the couple returned from the honeymoon he was his old somber self again. But presently a satisfied gleam shone in the green eyes. Tommy Cruse, at fifty, was going to be a father. He became one, ten months after the wedding day. At the same time, he became a widower. Was he inwardly disappointed that the child was not a boy who would be Thomas Cruse, Jr.? No one could tell. Was he shattered by the death in childbirth of the former Miss Carter? No one was sure about that, either.

What all Helena soon knew beyond doubt was that Colonel Cruse (he apparently acquired the title simultaneously with his bank) had a new passion, greater than his old one for gold: the doll-like, yellow-haired child named Mary Margaret Cruse, "Mamie" to him and to the town in general.

Among those who looked on with sentimental approval at this love of aging father for infant daughter was a young reporter for the Helena *Independent*, Martin Hutchens. It really was something to see, said Martin Hutchens in later years. In the morning, Colonel Cruse and Mamie riding down the gulch behind a pair of grays, the Colonel in broadcloth

55

and shiny silk hat, Mamie in beribboned ruffles and clutching a toy. Through the day, while the Colonel conducted business at his bank, Mamie playing on the floor beside his roll-top desk, the sunlight streaming through the window and onto her pretty hair. Then, the banking day done, a visit to the Montana Club, with the Colonel taking a glass or two and Mamie, feet tapping restlessly, waiting to do her much-applauded little specialty. As the time neared to go home, he lifted her onto the bar, where to the smiles and handclapping of the gentlemen present she danced a nimble clog. She was a small darling, all right. It became a ritual.

"A little sweet refreshment for the sweet little lady?" the bartender always asked.

"Just a drop, Joe," said the proud Colonel, and Mamie had her tiny swallow—it couldn't properly be called a drink—of crème de menthe.

Then into the victoria behind the grays and up to the fine brick house on Benton Avenue, with its mansard roof and gate-enclosed lawn with the iron flower pots, that the Colonel had bought from Mr. Carter, his late wife's brother. So handsome a home was no more than fitting for a leading citizen of a town that now boasted it was the richest, per capita, in all the land.

So went the idyll, tenderly regarded by the Colonel's fellow townsmen. But as 1893 moved toward spring, the fellow townsmen had other matters on their minds. The Panic of '93 was casting its long shadow, nowhere more ominously than here.

Like other major silver-producing States, Montana had rejoiced in 1890 when the Silver Purchase Act was passed, requiring the United States Government to buy four and a half million ounces of silver a month and issue against it paper notes that would be legal tender redeemable at the Treasury in silver or in gold. The silver producers were content. So, for another reason, were citizens by the million who, given their choice, turned in silver certificates for gold and hoarded it.

Colonel Cruse, in his snug little red brick bank, looked on and said nothing. The silver dollar was dropping. So was the federal gold reserve. The Silver Purchase Act was repealed by Congress, and that was the signal. In Last Chance Gulch nervous tremors blossomed into fear and then rage when the other two banks in Helena exploded in the faces of depositors who demanded their savings. Would the Thomas Cruse Savings Bank lend the Merchant's National a hand, officers of the Merchant's inquired? Colonel Cruse stared at them. His long memory went back to a day when he had wandered timidly into the Merchant's National and drawn a raucous hoot before he could get half way through his request for a grubstaking loan.

So there would be hell popping in Last Chance Gulch the next morning, young Martin Hutchens of the *Independent* suspected. At 8:30 A.M. he waited on a corner near Colonel Cruse's mansion. Would Mamie be riding as usual with her father that day, he wondered. Mamie would not. But there was Colonel Cruse, settling into his victoria. Never had his broadcloth been more neatly pressed, his silk hat shinier, the handsome grays more dashing.

The reporter followed the victoria down Last Chance Gulch. Before the closed doors of the Merchant's National a silent crowd packed the street from curb to curb. They parted for Colonel Cruse's carriage. He looked over their heads toward the ruined bank. He grinned.

That did it. The silence broke into a furious roar. Fists shook. Colonel Cruse kept grinning and waited for a break in the noise.

"Yez can come to my bank and get a loan," he shouted to such officers of the Merchant's National as might be there and listening. "At four per cent a month . . . as an accommodation," he added.

He settled back comfortably in the victoria and continued on his way to the Thomas Cruse Savings Bank. Arriving, he found a line of fretful depositors. The *Independent*'s reporter saw him frown, then grin again.

"Come in," he said genially to the depositors. They followed him into the bank and down to its cellar vaults. There, in dully gleaming gold behind iron bars, was $600,000 of his Drum Lummon money.

"Yez can have what's coming to yez if yez want it," he announced, "and with interest. I'm a sound money man myself."

Aware of what had happened to silver-backed currency, no depositor asked for his savings that day, or any other day, from Colonel Cruse.

From a State shaken by the Panic, young Martin Hutchens returned to his native East to be a New York and Chicago newspaperman before he came west again twenty-five years later. But the ancients reminiscing on the lawns of the Montana town of my boyhood went on with Thomas Cruse's story as if it were a succession of yesterdays. It is a way, I learned, that old-timers have.

His revenge obtained, they said, Colonel Cruse settled down to the pleasures of a non-incorporated man of means. He operated a ranch successfully. He drilled Montana's first oil well. He developed other mines, though none could ever mean to him what the Drum Lummon did. Save for the mighty copper magnates, William Andrews Clark and Marcus Daly, he was the state's richest man. And there was his beloved Mamie.

When they talked of Mamie, the old men looked away and spoke guardedly in the presence of a boy. Having grown into adolescence, Mamie was away a good deal, at school in the East and elsewhere. How much did the Colonel know about the life she led? The old men could only guess, but everybody else, they reckoned, knew or thought they knew. There were whispers of drugs and alcohol . . . started early, some said . . . the taste acquired as a child . . . those nips of liqueur at the Montana Club, a little darling's reward for the clog dancing on the bar. . . .

Whatever Colonel Cruse knew or did not know, he concentrated on business and the building of Helena's proposed new Roman Catholic cathedral. It was to be the pride of the Helena faithful, the greatest edifice of its kind between the Twin Cities and the Pacific Coast, and one and all were aware that it could not even have been thought of without the Colonel's contribution of $250,000. Then Mamie came home from what the local papers called "extensive travels," and on a November day in 1913 she died at twenty-seven after what the same papers called "several years of failing health."

You could tell by looking at him, the old men said, that Colonel Cruse cared very little after that about living. He held on, though, because there was St. Helena's Cathedral, nearing completion. It was ready for dedication a year after Mamie's death. He died a week after attending the dedication services, at which his fellow parishioners noticed—although as usual they pretended not to—that he held his prayer book upside down. The astute Colonel Cruse, triumphant miner, industrialist, banker, had never learned to read or write.

VIII

June Sunday, 1876

IN MONTANA THEY WERE ARGUING ABOUT HIM forty-odd years
after his last day, Sunday afternoon, June 25, 1876. They still
argue about him today, and about what he did or did not do
in the bleak hills beside the meandering Little Big Horn
River. Neither George Armstrong Custer, nor his Seventh
Cavalry, nor most of the Sioux and Cheyennes who destroyed him and some 270 of his men, were of Montana.
Nevertheless it was our battle, as surely as the Alamo be-
longs to Texas and Chancellorsville to Virginia. It had taken
place within our borders. It was not only the most crushing
defeat the United States Army had ever suffered at the hands
of the Indians, it contained an abiding mystery, the more
captivating because it promised never to be solved. Dead
men could not talk, and who could believe the testimony
of the victorious Indian survivors when they could not agree
among themselves?

"He was a son of a bitch!" said one of the old men one
afternoon.

Although I naturally had nothing to say about this, I
could not help being startled. My impression of Custer was
based on the painting—no saloon window was without it—
that advertised Anheuser-Busch beer: "Custer's Last Fight,"
with the long-haired hero, saber and pistol in hand, fighting

it out to the last amid smoke and fire and blood, altogether a noble figure. (I could not have been aware that his hair was close-cropped that day, and that no one in the battle carried a saber.) But if I was surprised, I noticed that even among the Custer-hating old man's companions a shaggy eyebrow or two rose slightly at his vehemence. Still, he went unchallenged, because after all he had fought on another part of the field that day as a trooper under Major Marcus A. Reno in the bitter engagement that preceded Custer's annihilation by an hour or two. Moreover, the old man, when a very young man, had served in Custer's Michigan Cavalry Brigade and later in the Third Cavalry Division in the last months of the War (there was no reason to identify *that* war) when Grant was closing in on Lee, and no cavalry was more dashing than that of the fierce young Ohioan with the yellow hair and the crimson cravat.

"I believed in him then. By God, I did," said the old man. "I believed in him so much I enlisted in the Seventh when they made him lieutenant colonel of it and sent him west to fight Indians. It lasted right up to Washita Creek."

The circle nodded understandingly. It was only later that I would appreciate the irony of what Custer's one-time admirer said next.

"Washita! Think of him making his name as an Indian fighter down there in the Indian Territory, wiping out a Cheyenne village, making off with a pretty squaw for himself, marching off and leaving Major Elliott and eighteen men to get killed and mutilated two miles away! Who was going to trust him after that?"

That was in 1868. Did the ghost of Major Elliott, I wondered, haunt Custer from then on? Perhaps not. He apparently could justify anything to himself, and, besides, he had other troubles. By 1876 he had won the enmity of President Grant by testifying against Grant's dishonest Secretary of War, thus launching a feud that reflected more on Grant than on Custer and in any case put him in need of a smashing triumph of some kind. Possibly, now, it was on the horizon.

For the Northern Cheyennes and the Sioux were on the warpath, in rebellion against the breaking of a treaty that had guaranteed them Western South Dakota as a reservation and a hunting ground. The white man's greedy rush into the Black Hills, when gold was discovered there in 1874, told the Indians what they could expect. The war drums were beating. Young braves on the reservations listened and took to the open country. Although ordered to return to the reservations by January 31, 1876, they stayed away. The United States Army planned a campaign to subdue them permanently.

So this was to be the big show-down, a three-pronged strategy that would entrap the Sioux and Cheyennes—General George Crook's column moving northwest from Fort Fetterman, in Wyoming; General John Gibbon moving down from Montana Territory with infantry and cavalry; General Alfred Terry starting west from Fort Lincoln, in Dakota Territory, with three companies of infantry and seven of cavalry, the latter under the immediate command of Custer. They would meet, if all went according to schedule, a little after mid-June where Rosebud Creek pours into the Yellowstone River, in South Central Montana. Somewhere in that vicinity the "hostiles" would be hemmed in and dealt with.

Was there, from the beginning, an air of impending disaster? The old Reno trooper was inclined to think so. It was a bleak, misty morning when the Seventh rode out of Fort Lincoln. The band made a brave show, playing the regimental march, "Garry Owen," and "The Girl I Left Behind," the latter a not exactly judicious selection; soldiers' and officers' wives were already crying enough. And then, he said, a strange, ominous thing happened. As the sun broke through the mist, the marching and riding men seemed also to be marching and riding in the sky as well—a mirage to chill the blood.

On June 21 the Seventh reached the mouth of the Rosebud, and on the afternoon of that day Terry, Gibbon and Custer met aboard the steamer *Far West* to go over the plan once more. General Crook was not present, for a significant reason of which his colleagues on the *Far West* were not as yet aware. General Crook's column, four days before, had been sent reeling by a Sioux-Cheyenne force fifty miles away in the headwaters of the Rosebud.

Still, what was left of the plan seemed sound. General Custer and his Seventh would proceed south up Rosebud Creek, following an Indian trail found by Major Reno and a scouting expedition. Presumably it would take him, as in fact it did, westward into the Little Big Horn Valley. Terry and Gibbon would go up the Yellowstone to the lower end of that valley. The trap was set. What could be neater, on paper?

"A trap!" said the old trooper, with the special bitterness of painful memory. "A trap for the hunter. There we were, starting off with a fancy review, Custer's boys headed up the Rosebud, riding past Custer, Gibbon and Terry, a lot of music and saluting. 'Don't be greedy,' Gibbon says to Custer, just before Custer moves to the head of the column. 'Leave some of those Indians for us.' Custer doesn't say anything at all. I wonder why I didn't think then there was something wrong, and later when we heard he'd turned down a chance to bring along Brisbin's Second Cavalry, from Montana. But no, it had to be nothing but the Seventh, because the Seventh was Custer, and Custer was the Seventh."

On they went, southwest up the Rosebud, riding hard, getting tired—except Custer, who never tired.

"That devil of his was riding him, like it did in the war back East," said the old trooper. "Glory—he had to have it. It made him a hell of a soldier then. Phil Sheridan said so.

Sheridan said he never had a better Cavalry officer. Now he was still under Sheridan, but the man he had his sights on was Grant. He was going to show Grant up, Grant who'd made him look bad in public."

Late on Saturday, June 24, they were near the divide that separates the valleys of the Rosebud and the Little Big Horn. An Indian trail, a big one, led west over the divide. The scouts, Indian and white, knew it. Custer knew it.

"We could have rested that night and the next day and attacked on the twenty-sixth but no, Custer has to order a forced march Saturday night and into Sunday morning. As soon as dawn breaks, our scouts see a big camp off to the north, across the Little Big Horn. They see Sioux scouts who see us, and head off north to carry the word. Bloody Knife, our Arikara scout—a great one, too—warns Custer. We haven't got enough bullets to take care of all those people down there, he says. Lonesome Charley Reynolds and Mitch Bouyer tell him the same thing, but Custer pays no attention to them. He says maybe Bouyer is a coward—Bouyer, the half-breed Sioux that Jim Bridger trained to be a scout!"

"Maybe Custer figured he'd be in trouble if he didn't attack right away, if he let those Indians get away," one of the old men ventured to suggest. "He'd have been court-martialed, sure."

Surprisingly, the old Reno trooper agreed. "All right, but then what the hell does he do? With a lot of Indians out ahead of us—God knows how many, maybe five thousand warriors —he divides up the command in three parts, three companies to Benteen, three to Reno, one to guard the pack train, five for himself; sends Benteen scouting the hell and gone off to the left across a couple of ridges, Reno down into the valley to charge the village. He tells Reno he'll support him, then goes off north with his five companies on the other side of the river from Reno, and that's the last we see of him alive."

"Maybe he figured on crossing back over the river and making a flank attack on the village while Reno was hitting it straight on," one of the old men suggested.

"God damn him! Why didn't he say so in the first place? I'll tell you something. He didn't have any plan at all. He was hoping for a grandstand play. He was thinking Indians wouldn't fight in daylight, just because he'd always caught 'em at night or in the dawn."

I had a fleeting impression that one ancient member of the audience, who had served in the Army of the Confederacy, was mildly amused by all this.

"Maybe Phil Sheridan's great officer wasn't such a great officer?" he offered.

"No," said the old trooper sadly, "he couldn't have been. Splitting up his command, underestimating the enemy. What kind of soldiering was that?"

So Reno's men, all 134 of them, and sixteen scouts, went on toward trouble, splashing across the stream now called Reno's Creek, fording the Little Big Horn, moving from a trot to a gallop, heading north to the Indian village in the valley. Did Custer think the Indians were running away from Reno's charge? Was it then he decided to attack from the flank or behind the Indian forces instead of supporting Reno from the rear?

"Whatever he was thinking, the battle was all over then, and don't let anybody who wasn't there tell you different," said the old trooper. "Oh, yes, we started off fine, going two miles before we saw a hostile. 'Thirty days furlough to the man who gets the first scalp!' yells a lieutenant named Varnum. The green kids in the battalion set up a cheer. Then the ground sprouts Indians, I swear it does, five hundred of them a quarter of a mile away, two hundred more moving around our left flank. Reno gives the order to dismount, form a skirmish line, and use a prairie dog town for breastworks. The line's too thin. Reno orders a withdrawal to a stand of timber near the river. We get back there all right, but it's too tough there, too, one of us against ten of them, and Reno orders another pull-back, across the Little Big Horn and up onto the bluffs on the east side of it.

"They keep saying Reno lost his head when he called for that retreat. We'd have been butchered to the last man if he hadn't, like Bloody Knife, shot between the eyes, and his blood and brains spattering all over Reno's face, a couple of feet away, and the wounded and the horses screaming. All those magazine writers and books that said we should have stayed there and taken the pressure off Custer—why didn't he back us up and take the pressure off us?"

No one seemed to have any conclusive answer to that. No one, as I was to realize in due course, had any conclusive answer to anything at all about the Battle of the Little Big Horn. Every foot and every second of it were going to be debated forever.

The old trooper, holding forth so bitterly and so combatively while his friends listened this day, was one of the lucky ones. Shot in his left forearm, and his horse killed and downed, he held on with his right hand to the stirrup of another trooper's horse, was dragged across the Little Big Horn, and made his way up the hill under the fire of snipers.

"Along comes Benteen then, with his three companies that had been off on that scouting expedition to the south, and it was a good thing they arrived, or we'd have been finished off the way Custer and his five companies were getting it about then, though we didn't know that. You think we should have gone to help Custer? Yes, if you read what was written later. Right then, we thought he should have come to help us. There was gunfire down the valley, five miles or so away. That had to be Custer. We thought he'd won, of course, and gone on, maybe to join Gibbon and Terry at the north end of the valley and claim the victory, and the hell with us, the way he left Major Elliott in the lurch at Washita."

The survivors would never forget it, that Sabbath night and most of the next day on the Reno-Benteen hill, the wounded moaning and calling for water—water that was near by and yet far away, because the Indians were drawing a bead on anyone venturing from the bluffs down to the Little Big Horn. Fifteen men finally got to the river with canteens and kettles, for which they and four sharpshooters covering them were later awarded Congressional Medals of Honor. The Indian snipers' fire dropped onto the hilltop during the night, and an Indian attack at dawn was beaten off. As Monday drew to an end the huge Indian encampment moved south, trailing off through the valley toward the Big Horn Mountains in Wyoming. A trick, possibly? The Reno and Benteen battalions stayed where they were, up on their hill, through Monday night and into Tuesday morning, when for the first time they learned from an advance party of the Terry-Gibbon force of the fate of Custer and five companies of the Seventh on the desolate slope downstream beside the Little Big Horn.

"Custer licked! We couldn't believe it," said the old trooper. "Whatever they thought of Custer, men on that hill broke down and bawled when they heard what happened to friends of theirs who died with him. The ones that died quick were lucky. The ones wounded and dying slow, they had their heads bashed in with stone clubs, the squaws and Indian kids coming up later with knives."

The old trooper was assigned to the burial party, and it was not something he cared to remember, but he did remember it because he could not possibly forget it. The stripped bodies had been a day and a half under the Montana sun, and the flies had been at work.

"From a mile or so away, they looked like white boulders," he said, "but when you got closer there was no mistaking. A lot of them had arrows sticking in them. The best guns the Indians had were better than our single-shot Springfields, but they used the bow and arrow too—a good weapon to shoot out of a gulch with; had a high trajectory; an Indian could let it go and stay hidden."

The work that burial party was assigned to was enough to turn a man's stomach, he said, and the gravediggers didn't pretend to do a very good job in that thin, rocky soil. God only knew what a time the wolves had there when the living departed. As for Custer, the old trooper went on, anticipating a question, he wasn't cut up the way some others were. One bullet hole in the head, one in the chest, and, no, there was no indication of suicide, though who would blame him if he had taken his own life? Always save the last bullet for yourself, the old saying went on the Indian-fighting frontier, out of bitter knowledge of the Indians' way with prisoners.

"What I blame him for was something else!" the old trooper barked in an agony of recollection. "The whole thing shouldn't have happened like it did! It had to be a tough fight, but it could have gone the other way if it hadn't been for Custer wanting to be a Goddamn hero! Somebody'll tell the truth about it, but they won't while Mrs. Custer's still alive."

The old trooper was not entirely accurate about that. Custer's critics—Captain Benteen, notably—managed to make themselves heard during Mrs. Custer's lifetime, which continued into the 1930's, more than half a century after her husband's death. Yet it certainly is true that her long, loving idealization of him, in books and articles and interviews, created an enduring legend; that, and the romantic Anheuser-Busch painting. It was only by chance, on one of those summer lawn afternoons in Missoula, that I heard another side of the story.

For that matter, it was by chance that on a day in the 1950's, in New York City, I heard from Miss Marguerite Merington, veteran actress and a companion of Mrs. Custer's later years, about a curious moment they experienced together.

June Sunday, 1876

Invited to Montana in 1926 to attend the battlefield ceremonies commemorating the fiftieth anniversary of Custer's Last Stand, Mrs. Custer declined. She chose instead to listen in her New York hotel room to a radio program on which the battle was re-enacted with extraordinarily vivid sound effects. The program faded out with a few scattered gunshots, followed by an aching silence. In the hotel room where Mrs. Custer had been listening there was also a silence. It finally was broken when she said, with an equanimity that startled Miss Merington: "Well, I suppose that's about the way it was."

Great Indian

THERE WERE INDIANS and then there were Indians, the old men used to say, much as they might have said that there were white men and then there were white men—in short, there was no generalizing about people in the mass. You could hate the Sioux because they were cruel, the man who had served with Reno suggested one afternoon, adding that maybe you hated the Sioux because you feared them, but at least you did not despise them, as even other Indians despised the Digger Indians, for instance, who lived on roots and grasshoppers down in the Nevada-Utah desert.

About one Indian and his tribe the veterans had no qualifications whatever. Chief Joseph, of the Nez Percés, was a great chief and a fine man, and his people were a noble race.

"Now this is probably a hell of a thing to say," the old Reno trooper went on, "and I wouldn't have said it not so long ago, but it's a fact. After the Little Big Horn, I went over from the Seventh Cavalry into Gibbon's Seventh Infantry, and the next summer when Joseph broke loose from the reservation and headed off through Idaho and Montana for Canada we chased him upward of eighteen hundred miles before he got pinned down thirty miles this side of the border, up in the Bearpaw Mountains. What I mean is, I'm sorry he didn't get away. He should have. He deserved to."

The old man sat back for a moment, as if expecting lightning to strike, perhaps a bolt launched from Valhalla by that implacable enemy of the western American Indian, William Tecumseh Sherman.

When nothing happened, he said, "Here's these Nez Percés, never shed a drop of white blood till 1877, great friends of Lewis and Clark seventy years or so before, tall, big-boned, handsome people, and the best looking of them all was Joseph. The government gives them a fine reservation in the Wallowa Valley in Oregon, but you know what happens then. It always happened. The land's too good, so the whites want it, the way they wanted the Black Hills after gold was discovered there and the Sioux got pushed out. Even so, Joseph's ready to give in and move to another place, the Lapwai reservation in Idaho. He knows it's not so good, but he doesn't want a lot of bloodshed. Then three of his young braves go wild and kill a few whites, and he knows the whites will say it's his fault, though it isn't, so there's nothing for him and his people to do but get out of there the best way they can, off to Canada."

How the peace-loving Chief Joseph, with no military experience whatever, escaped from Oregon with some two hundred warriors and four hundred women, children and old men, whipping General O. O. Howard's Federal forces in two battles in Idaho and taking off for Montana across the Bitter Root Mountains and through the Lolo Pass—this was only the beginning of his astounding flight toward freedom.

"Joseph lived a long time and he never had much to laugh about, by and large," said the old trooper, "but once in a while he must have laughed inside till he was fit to bust. He gets to about where Lolo Pass comes into the Bitter Root Valley, and there's a U.S. Army captain from Fort Missoula who's put up a lot of logs that he calls a barricade, like he's going to stop Joseph with *that*.

" 'Surrender your arms or you'll cross here only over our dead bodies,' this captain says. Charles Rawn, his name is.

" 'We'll cross the mountains, and not over any dead bodies,' says Joseph, and, just so, he takes his force around the end of Rawn's lines and over a hill into the Bitter Root Valley without a shot, and moves on south, like Captain Rawn was a child tugging at his sleeve. I swear I almost felt sorry for the captain when I heard about it, the way people laughed and gave his barricade a name it's still got, Fort Fizzle.

"Colonel Gibbon, though, doesn't think anything's so funny while his Seventh Infantry comes marching over from Fort Shaw, near Helena, six companies of us and a wagon train, into Missoula and on down the Bitter Root Valley, chasing Joseph. For one thing, the civilians in the valley tell us Joseph's a mighty good Indian. He doesn't bother anybody. He sees to it the women don't have anything to worry about from his warriors. When he comes to a settlement he pays for what he wants, including guns and ammunition. Funny what a spot of cash will do sometimes, isn't it? Makes a man think twice about glory. The Missoula citizen militia decides there's no danger, after all, since Joseph's moving off in another direction from their town, and most of them head for home. Gibbon hollers about this, but what can he do?"

But Colonel John Gibbon, professional soldier, kept going, as a soldier should, and eventually he had his chance. On the afternoon of August 8, 1877, his scouts located the Nez Percés, camped in a meadow beside Ruby Creek on the eastern slope of the Continental Divide. Unsuspecting, knowing that General Howard was far behind but not knowing that Colonel Gibbon and the Seventh Infantry were approaching, the Indians were enjoying themselves with feasting and footraces. Gibbon's scouts reported to him, several miles back along the trail, and the Colonel hatched a sound plan. He ordered a day's rations and ninety rounds of ammunition for his men and marched them by night to within a few hundred yards of the Indian camp, where they lay in the brush and waited for the dawn. When the first light came, they attacked.

"By all the rules," said the old cavalryman-turned-infantry-man, "that should have been the end of it. We caught them cold and asleep, the way Custer caught the Cheyennes at Washita. We tore through their village, clubbing and shooting, and we'd have burned it too, if the dew hadn't made the tepees too damp. But that Chief Joseph, he didn't follow the rules. He wouldn't let himself get routed. In a few minutes he and his two main chiefs, Looking Glass and White Bird, were rallying their band and fighting back. They were cross-firing us from the thickets and the river bank. They had marksmen like no other Indians you ever saw, even the kids and women. Pretty soon we were retreating back up the hill we'd started from, up in the timber above the meadow, and we were digging in to save our lives. The Indians were coming back into their village, and the noise they made when they found their old people and kids dead in the tepees was something to raise the gooseflesh.

"So there we were, the side that was supposed to win in a hurry, but now it's us that's under siege, and just to make it worse the Nez Percés capture a howitzer and two thousand rounds of ammunition coming up with a pack train.

"They picked us off all day and into the night from behind trees and boulders. They started a grass fire that would have burned us out if the wind hadn't changed. Our rations ran out, and the only way to get water was to sneak through the Indian lines to Ruby Creek. You were taking your chances. But now I'll tell you something people couldn't hardly believe later. The morning comes, and the battle's over, with the Indians all gone. We go out to bury our dead, and not a single one is scalped. Joseph wouldn't allow it."

The old soldier certainly was not telling his listeners, except for myself, anything of which they were not already aware. The character of Chief Joseph, the epic of a campaign fought with all the odds against him, was an old, proud Montana story. That he was an Oregonian and not a Montanan mattered not at all. Because his great feat had taken place largely within our State, he—like the Battle of the Little Big Horn—belonged to us. The old soldier's audience no more tired of hearing the story once more than children object to still another rendering of a Robin Hood tale.

He was going on about it, saying, "You remember the damnedest strange things. On that long day of the battle, the ninth of August, there I was, flattened out in a shallow rifle pit hoping some Nez Percé sharpshooter up in a tree somewhere wouldn't see me, when I looked around and saw one of those citizen volunteers who hadn't gone home, fellow by the name of Luther Johnson. I could just see the top of his head. How in hell did he get down there, I asked him. Seemed he'd prospected for gold here ten years before, and stumbled right into a hole he'd dug way back then. It came in mighty handy. When things got quieter, I went back toward the command post, and there's Colonel Gibbon with a wound in his thigh. He was a good man, that Gibbon, but I couldn't help thinking even then that some day he wasn't going to be happy about this Battle of the Big Hole. A man that fought at Antietam and helped hold the center on the last day at Gettysburg, and went on to the Wilderness and Spotsylvania—how good is he going to feel about a battle where we kill thirty warriors and eighty women and children? I never felt so proud of my part in it, though I swear to God I never killed a woman or a child. Joseph didn't either, and he could have killed a lot of them if he'd wanted to, when you think of the chances he had, all those white settlements he marched past.

"Well, now, there he is, moving off to the south and dipping over into Idaho again, leaving Howard and Gibbon to pull themselves together and decide what to do next. Joseph gets to Camas Meadows and camps there. Howard's cavalry is chasing him and goes into camp eighteen miles away from Joseph. Along about twilight, just when Howard is feeling safe, about forty of Joseph's young men are tearing into his mule herd, cutting out about a hundred and fifty of 'em. Then Joseph double-flanks three companies of cavalry sent out to chase him, as he figures they would be, and then he's off to the east again, this time into Wyoming. He's gained three days on Howard, who misses those pack mules. Some of Joseph's young men come across a party of tourists in Yellowstone Park, and rough up the white gentlemen in the group, but Joseph sees to it that the ladies get away safe. I tell you, he was a decent man. Now he's going north up across the Yellowstone River, moving fast before Colonel Samuel Sturgis, and what's been put together of Custer's old Seventh Cavalry, can come over from Fort Keogh and stop him."

They tried to stop him at what would be remembered as the Battle of Canyon Creek. Again he outflanked them and sent them off in the wrong direction by an almost comic device: his warriors tied sagebrush to their lariats, stirred up dust off to the south, and drew Howard's troops away from Joseph's main command. So Joseph got away to the north once more, though he lost five hundred wornout ponies to the Federal troops and their always obliging Indian allies, the Crows, a tribe whose medicine men must have told them that one day the white man would triumph and they would do well to be on the winning side.

Having outthought and outfought various elements of the United States Army, Joseph's force headed up the Musselshell River, went around the west side of the Judith Mountains, and crossed the Missouri River below Fort Benton. He seized stores recently unloaded from a river steamer from St. Louis, inadequately guarded by a dozen soldiers and a few private citizens. The road to the border and freedom seemed clear now—up through the buffalo country, beyond the Bearpaw Mountains. He could afford to pause, as he thought then and said later, and let the old people and the children rest. He was mistaken.

Cutting northwest from Fort Keogh, with 350 cavalrymen and infantrymen, was that ambitious and frequently frustrated Civil War veteran and Indian fighter, Colonel Nelson A. Miles. Keeping the Little Rockies between his force and Joseph's, he completed a forced march of 200 miles and, Joseph having failed to put out scouts in the direction from which Miles came, the Colonel caught the Chief unprepared. Again, as at the Big Hole, Joseph should have been routed, and was not. Miles' cavalry charged confidently and was stopped. Nez Percé sharpshooters, holding their fire until it was most effective, picked off bluecoated officers at an appalling rate. A second cavalry charge failed. The Indians dropped back to ravines behind their camp, dug trenches, and awaited a siege that was to end only when hunger, a blizzard, and Miles' artillery reduced Joseph's already ravaged band to despair. Howard and his force came up from the south, Colonel Miles regarding the general with bare civility until Howard promised that it would be Miles who accepted Joseph's surrender.

"You can be damn sure that Howard's arrival had something to do with Joseph's decision to surrender," said the old soldier on this afternoon almost half a century later. "Howard and Gibbon between them had a hell of a lot more to do with wearing Joseph down, in three months over eighteen hundred miles, than Nelson A. Miles did in five days after a two-hundred-mile march with a fresh command against a lot of tired Indians. But I'll tell you something. It doesn't matter much who took Joseph's surrender. It was the way he surrendered.

"Name me a greater speech," the old man said challengingly, "than the one he made that day he handed over his rifle to Miles. I can hear it now, the way the interpreter talked it off."

He closed his eyes and recited, from memory:

I am tired of fighting. Our chiefs are killed. Looking
Glass is dead. Toohulhulsate is dead. The old men are all
dead. He who led the young men is dead. It is cold and we
have no blankets. The little children are freezing to death.
My people, some of them, have run away to the hills and
have no blankets, no food. No one knows where they are—
perhaps freezing to death. I want to have time to look for
my children and see how many of them I can find. Maybe
I shall find them among the dead. Hear me, my chiefs. I
am tired. My heart is sick and sad. From where the sun now
stands I will fight no more, forever.

"He was the best man on the field that day," said the old
man, emerging with a kind of ferocity from his recitation,
"and don't you ever forget it," although, as far as I could see,
no one appeared on the point of arguing with him about it.
"Miles promised Joseph he could go back to Idaho, and you
have to believe Miles meant it, but of course nothing came of
that promise. Even as great an Indian as Joseph was sure to
wind up with the dirty end of the stick. Miles' Cheyenne
and Sioux scouts even got their pick of the Nez Percé horses.
The Nez Percés, the best Indians you ever saw, went off to
Fort Leavenworth in Kansas, where malaria killed more of
them than Miles, Howard and Gibbon ever did.

" 'The Great Spirit Chief who rules above seemed to be
looking the other way,' Joseph says. From there they go to
the Indian Territory, which isn't any healthier. After eight
years, what's left of them get back to the Northwest, where
Joseph lives on till 1904 when he dies on the Colville Reservation in Washington. He keeps asking the government for just
a little piece of his old homeland in the Wallowa Valley in
Oregon, but do you suppose those greedy bastards who took
over when he was driven out in the 1870's would let him have
anything at all? You suppose right.

"He goes to New York City for the big show dedicating

77

Grant's Tomb. He gives a speech at the University of Washington in Seattle. He sits for portraits by painters and sculptors. A year after he dies, some historical society puts up a fine marble monument over his grave at Nespelem, State of Washington."

The old man paused, and shook his head.

"And to think I might have shot him that day, August 9, 1877, at The Battle of the Big Hole—me, a crazy young soldier, all hot for battle. I probably would have, too, if I'd had a chance, and I'd have spent the rest of my life, after I got some sense, trying to tell myself it was an accident."

At the supper table that evening, when I reported the gist of my old friend's discourse, my father's smile was one of reminiscence and pleasure.

"Your old soldier was right about Joseph," said my father. "I saw Joseph, and there never was a greater Indian. I could count on five fingers the people I ever met who had half his dignity."

Here was a fact of my father's life that I had never heard. Had he been, among other things, an Indian fighter? But he was still too young to have been that.

My father laughed. "I was a reporter," he said, "writing for Mr. Pulitzer's New York *World* about the parade up Riverside Drive one day in April, 1897, when Grant's Tomb was dedicated. There was a lot of oratory, which I'm glad to say I've forgotten. I'll tell you what I'll never forget, though— Chief Joseph riding up the Drive with Buffalo Bill. There they were, the Old West, side by side."

The *World*'s city editor, it appeared, had sensibly assigned a sometime Montanan to cover Chief Joseph's New York visit.

My father said, "He put up at the Astor House, and he wore his full regalia, and even New Yorkers who'd never been off Manhattan Island could see that here was a great

78

man. Well, maybe not every New Yorker. There was one, a newspaperwoman, I'm sorry to say, who came to interview him. She was wearing a fancy hat all covered with birds or fruit or something. She asked Joseph, through an interpreter, 'Did you ever scalp anybody?'

"Joseph came as close to smiling as I saw him come during that whole week. He looked at her hat. He said to the interpreter, 'Tell her that I have nothing in my collection as fine as that.'

"How could anybody help but respect a man like Joseph?" my father continued. "He didn't want to fight, but when he did he was what Miles called him, the Napoleon of the American Indians. American troops slaughtered his women and children, but he wouldn't allow atrocities in return. In that last battle in the Bearpaw Mountains, the Nez Percés even went between the lines and gave water to wounded soldiers. And that surrender speech of his—if you want to know something about style, memorize it and learn something."

A person could always learn something, I was discovering, if he listened carefully.

All in all, it had been quite a day.

Just the Same, a Lady

LISTENING TO THE OLD MEN on the lawn, it occurred to me one day that if they—who had experienced so much at first hand—could frequently disagree about this or that person or event, how was some Montana historian to arrive in the future at what he knew to be the truth? The day on which I came to this conclusion was the one on which they got around to recalling Calamity Jane. In the heat of their discussion they fortunately forgot all about the wide, tender, young ears listening just outside their circle.

"A whore," said one old man in a soft, even, but disapproving tone.

"Yes, but a hell of a lot more," said another. His face reddened with anger, and I thought I saw him tightening his grip on his cane, as I had seen him do once or twice before, notably when the generalship of Ulysses S. Grant was questioned by the sole ex-Confederate in the group. "A good woman," he said. "Do you hear me? She made her living the way a girl did, following soldiers and railroad construction men around and about. What's that got to do with it? She had a good heart. Do you understand?"

Calamity Jane's critic was retreating but was not entirely routed. "Which Calamity are we talking about?"

"*Which* Calamity?" Her old admirer appeared dumfounded.

"That's right. A lot of women claimed to be Calamity."

"I'm talking," said the admirer, "about the Calamity Jane that came out of Missouri in about 'sixty-four, Martha Jane Cannary she called herself, thirteen years old or thereabouts. I saw her in Alder Gulch, looking after a young brother and sister, begging in the streets, because their mother was a whore, and a bad one too, and their old man was a tinhorn gambler that was lucky not to get shot. What was a girl going to do?"

"There were those said her real name was Mary Jane Dalton and she was born near Fort Laramie, and her father a soldier," said the critic. "She had kind of red hair, and she was pretty."

"She had black hair," said the admirer, "and she wasn't hardly pretty. She had high cheek bones, almost like an Indian, and I'll tell you how plain-looking she was—when she was a teamster with General Crook in the 'seventy-six campaign against the Sioux, wearing those old buckskins of hers, it was two weeks before anybody learned she was a woman. She could shoot with any ordinary soldier, and she could crack a whip over a span of mules so loud you could hear it in the next canyon. She could talk to 'em, too. It singed your ears."

There followed a mild dispute about the origin of her nickname: whether it was because she had a tendency to raise hell when she was drunk, or because she hurried to take care of the sick when calamity, in the form of an epidemic, struck at some frontier town with sudden, terrible results, as epidemics did.

It was in her role as ministering angel that she acquired that name, the admirer declared positively. He had reason to know this, and presently it was clear why he would hear no harsh word about Martha Jane Cannary. In 1878 he was prospecting outside Deadwood, in the Black Hills, when smallpox swept that settlement. It was a dark time for a dozen victims laid up in a cabin with one doctor and no nurse to look after them—no nurse, that is, until Calamity turned up and allowed she would help out. She would likely get small-pox herself, the doctor said, and he added—because he and she could be frank with each other—that the scars it left would do her no good in the profession she intermittently followed. Overhearing this conversation, the afflicted listened anxiously. It made no difference, said Calamity. She would stay, and she did, and only a couple of the patients died. She did not get smallpox, and she went on her way unscarred.

"Now," said the old admirer, "do you know what I mean by a good heart? I'm not taking anything away from the doctor, but the ones that got out of there alive, we wouldn't have done it without *her*."

There was a silence as of agreement.

The scars Calamity bore were of another kind. At forty, with eleven years remaining to her, she was an old woman and a drunkard. Persuaded by well-meaning friends that a touch of big city civilization might reform her, she went way back East to Chicago and supported herself by appearing in a carnival sideshow. She stood this humiliating freakishness as long as she could, and came back to be a nuisance in a West rapidly becoming too respectable for women like herself.

One of the old men said that, now he came to think of it, a son-in-law of his had known Calamity, a cowboy who wound up dead broke one day in the '80's in Miles City, capital of Montana's cattle industry. He borrowed four bits from Calamity for a meal and said he'd pay her when he could. She didn't give a damn whether he did or not, said Calamity. The next time he saw her, fifteen years later, he handed her a half dollar. Calamity was angry. Hadn't she said she didn't give a damn if she never got it back? They had a drink together with the fifty cents, and the cowboy kidded her a little about having gone back East to get civilized. To his embarrassment, Calamity began to cry. "Why don't the sons of bitches leave me alone and let me go to hell my own way?" she asked. He never saw her again.

Deadwood, though, saw a good deal more of her—more than it wanted to, because she had a way of roistering in the streets at hours when sober citizens were trying to sleep. Anyone else would have been locked up, but the old-timers, who cherished her as a vestige of their past, would allow no such indignity to be inflicted on Calamity. What did it matter, by that time, which of the stories about her were authentic and which were not? It certainly was to be doubted that Wild Bill Hickok ever was in love with her, a somewhat battered prostitute, but quite possibly she was in love with him, the still dashing Prince of Pistoleers. Maybe it really was true that she cornered his cowardly murderer, Jack McCall, with a butcher knife on that August day in 1876 when Bill carelessly sat with his back to an open door during a poker game in a Deadwood saloon.

"I'll go along with that story because I want to believe it," said her admirer in the circle on the lawn. "It's something she *might* have done, you see? And I like to think of her lying up there in the grave next to Bill's in the Deadwood cemetery." *Mt. Moriah Cemetery*

"One of her husbands was a fellow called Burke," said her critic. "I always heard she had eleven others, an even dozen all in all. And how many kids?"

"Who cares?" the admirer snapped. Perhaps, sick and grateful, he himself had fallen in love with Calamity in that pesthouse outside Deadwood in 1878? I was almost sure of it when he went on to say, "I wish to God I'd been with her when she died in 1903, up in that little mining camp in the Black Hills, place by the name of Terry." *50 miles from*

"Died of inflammation of the bowels, didn't she?" the critic *Deadwood* asked.

The hand tightened again on the cane.

"Call it pneumonia. She was a lady."

When, that evening, I reported this exchange, my father listened without speaking, and then offered an observation. "If you remember what you heard today about Calamity, you have learned something valuable. There were a lot of them out here like Calamity, part good, part bad, but more good than bad. Most people aren't all of a piece, and a good thing, too. They wouldn't be very interesting if they were."

More Than One Way to
Journey's End

Even a boy could soon realize that the true aristocrats of Montana were those who arrived there in the 1860's, or before, and stayed. That they may never have achieved anything resembling fame or wealth mattered not at all. Indeed, some of them had scorn—not, I remain certain, based on envy —for the more affluent later-comers, the promoters, the fast, big money-makers. Those early ones were the pioneers, in the most literal sense. They did it the hard way. A man or woman who reached Montana by covered wagon, or by steamer from St. Louis to Fort Benton, looked back with a special pride on that journey to a new world, a new life. No Pullman cushions, no steam-drawn cars, for *them*.

But even among those argonauts, I came to see, there was a division. Who was entitled to the greater pride, those who had come by covered wagon or those who had come by the always eccentric and dangerous Missouri River? My ancient friends used to discuss this at length, comparing—not always amicably—their memories. In imagination I would go along with them, sometimes across the plains and then again by river steamer, never quite deciding which route I myself would have preferred. It was better, I thought, that I did not really have to choose one way or the other.

"You had it easy, loafing around on a boat, St. Louis to Fort Benton," one old man would say.

"The hell we did," a river traveler would answer. "Those boats could blow up. They got stuck on sand bars. While we were still sitting on the sand bars, the Sioux or Blackfeet were popping at us from the bluffs."

"If you'd ever been with a covered-wagon train that got ambushed by Indians, you'd have known what a fight was," the across-the-plains veteran would say.

Then he would go on to tell what he remembered of it, and for a while at least I would be on his side of the argument and a member of his company. It would be a company that set out from the jumping-off place, Independence, Missouri, in a dozen prairie schooners heading away on what had once been the Oregon Trail, later the California Trail. There would be perhaps a hundred of us, with an old-time guide and wagon boss in charge. We would live chiefly on smoked side bacon, beans, dried fruit, rice and coffee, and whatever game we could find along the way. The prairie schooners would roll across the Nebraska plains, like great ships finding their way through a motionless sea. We would have our bad days, the schooners crashing down bluffs as they approached a ford on the North Platte. Women would shriek and children cry, and all along the way there would be reminders of those who had gone before but never got there, the shallow, unmarked graves with wolf tracks around them. . . .

"The cholera," a survivor said now. "God A'mighty, how it hit a man! He'd be feeling fine in the morning, and in the afternoon he'd be dead and buried, and we'd move on. There must have been five thousand of them in graves from Independence to Fort Laramie. But at night, if you didn't want to go crazy, you'd try to forget about who died that day. There'd be the wagons pulled up in a circle to make a corral, the fire going, and somebody with a fiddle playing 'Annie Laurie' while we sang. That was good. I'll never forget it."

"You'd see the damnedest things," said another, "like the

junk left along the trail where the going was hardest, every-thing from hairpins to pianos. I saw an Irishman going out of Independence pushing a wheelbarrow of stuff, heading for California. I saw a lot more, coming back. That Nebraska alkali burned the shoes off their feet. They'd seen the Ele-phant—they were scared, and I never blamed them."

"Women did better than a lot of the men. Had better nerves."

"They did, and that's a fact. A woman had a baby, the train held up for a few hours, and the next day she was riding along in one of those wagons that bounced around in the wheel ruts. Now and then one of them would go crazy, a baby dying, or maybe just the heat and the flies. But a woman who could shoot was as good as a man when the Indians closed in on a train."

"She saved the last bullet for herself, if it came to that."

The old men went into one of their significant silences. What happened to a woman taken prisoner by some, if not all, Indian tribes was a gruesome aspect of frontier history.

Again I fancied myself in that westering company. Through the alkali and dust of Nebraska, across the little rivers, up the steep bluffs, on our way to the rich, grassy uplands of South Pass, an easy climb to the top of the Con-tinental Divide, almost before we knew it. A major point, this one. From here on, all waters would be flowing toward the Pacific. We who were bound for Montana were almost there. There would be some rough desert to get through before we reached Fort Hall, Idaho, but nothing like the stretch that folks going on to California would have to cover after Fort Hall, that Nevada wilderness on the way to Hum-boldt Wells, bleak as the scarred face of the moon. North, then, from Fort Hall, up through the valley of the Snake River, across wide prairie land, the Tetons off to the east going purple in the sunset. Over the Continental Divide again, this time into Montana Territory. Presently we would be trending west toward the new gold field, the place called Bannack. We would know we were nearing it when we saw a sign saying "Tu Grass Hop Per digins 30 myle kepe the trale next the bluffe." And then, miraculously, we would be there, in that raucous little camp where every other foot of land along Grasshopper Creek was overturned and quartz miners were burrowing into the low hills on either side of it.

Maybe the first person I would see would be Sheriff Henry Plummer himself, chatting pleasantly with the citizens whom he was even then planning to rob and, if necessary, order murdered. . . .

However, there was much to be said also for that trip by water. Those who had taken the trip said so.

Having made the plains-and-mountains crossing to Bannack, I was back in St. Louis, on the waterfront in the early 1860's, ready to board a shallow-draft stern- or side-wheeler for Fort Benton, 2200 miles away, as far as a steamer could go up the Missouri. It was a spring morning, when the water was high, as it had to be if a boat was to skim over all those sand bars that lay ahead. The steamer, preferably, would be the *Luella*, with Captain Grant Marsh in the pilot house, he who in 1876 was to carry the wounded down the Yellowstone in his speedy *Far West* after the Battle of the Little Big Horn. Captain Marsh could take a river steamer across a light dew, his crew always said. A whistle blew, the last good-byes were shouted, the last tears of farewell shed. . . .

But the old man who had chosen to take a boat trip, rather than a prairie schooner trip, way back then, was talking again.

"Well, all right, it may have been easier than the plains," he conceded, somewhat reluctantly. "I guess you could even say it was a fine time. Deck passage for one hundred fifty dollars, a cabin for four hundred dollars, and the company as lively as you please." The passenger list, he observed, had a certain interesting variety—army officers and their wives on their way to far-off posts, ladies of another sort setting out to ply their trade in woman-hungry places where they could not fail to be appreciated, gamblers, would-be miners with dreams of impossible riches shining in their eyes, merchants, missionaries.

"A young man like me didn't have much chance to get lonesome," said the old man with an air of happy reminiscence. "Down on the deck, passengers like me slept in any kind of weather, cooked our own food, helped out when we stopped to wood up for fuel, even got a shot at a buffalo. What else could I ask for?

"If I'd had any brains," he went on, "I'd have stayed on the river, at least till the railroads came along in the 'eighties and took over the freighting business. A man with some money, enough to buy or build a twenty-thousand-dollar boat, he could double it on one round trip, St. Louis to Fort Benton and back. Ten to fifteen cents a pound for four hundred tons of cargo. How could you lose, if the Sioux didn't get you or a busted boiler blow you up? A good pilot like Grant Marsh got two–three thousand for a round trip, and he earned it. That river changed from one hour to the next. Maybe I could have been a pilot. But no, it had to be Alder Gulch for me, and no good claims left for a greenhorn by the time I got there."

Now I was on that boat with him, as I had been on a wagon train winding its way up the North Platte. At night we tied up along the bank—even a pilot like Grant Marsh wasn't apt to run his ship on that river after dark except in extraordinary circumstances. There were guitars playing, and dancing at night in the cabins, and card games, and good food, along with the fish you caught in the river or deer you shot from on deck. There would come a time when the Sioux threatened, and then we'd anchor in midstream, with sheet iron around the pilot house to protect us from Indian fire, because —thanks to the business that traders did with the Indians

89

—the Indians had repeating rifles that were better than the white man's, as Custer's Seventh Cavalry would learn at the Little Big Horn.

"God A'mighty," the old man was saying, "what a trip that was for an Ohio boy like me, right from the flat Midwest! Here I was, going up the same river Lewis and Clark followed. It wanders and it straggles, and for long spell it creeps along through country flat as a buckwheat cake back home. Then all of a sudden you're on the Upper Missouri and looking at sandstone cliffs you'd swear were castles, three hundred feet up from the water, with a mountain sheep standing on top of a turret, right there against the sunset. A lucky shot might get him, but I wasn't of a mind to shoot him, seeing him like that, and anyhow he was apt to scamper down that cliff faster than a gunsight could follow him. We'd do thirty–forty miles a day, and that was fast enough for me, no matter how anxious I was to get to Alder Gulch and all that gold."

He was even tempted, the old man said, to stay on for a while in Fort Benton when they finally got there, six weeks out of St. Louis. In fact, he did stay on for a week or so, long enough to see something of a town that was not quite like any other in Montana's history.

A dozen river packets tied up to a mile-long levee, some of them preparing to go down river with as much as two tons of raw gold dust. Bull trains laden with mining machinery, whiskey and tobacco for the mining camps in Western Montana, and north over the Whoop-Up Trail to Fort Macleod in Canada. Northwest Royal Mounted Police in their scarlet uniforms, French-Canadian trappers in their red sashes, greasy and ill-smelling wolfers, and the last of the mountain men in their buckskins—they must have been a sight to see along that single street in Fort Benton, lined with saloons and hurdy-gurdy houses. Walk in the middle of the street and tend to your own business if you want to stay out of trouble, the local slogan went.

"There were maybe twenty little cabins and houses, downstream from the old American Fur Company fort," said the old man. "The garbage, smelling like hell, was waiting in the street for somebody to throw it into the river, and people like Liver Eating Johnson were hanging around that would just as soon kill you as look at you. I was glad to get out of there, but I was glad I waited a bit, because I saw something I like to think of."

What, I wondered, was that?

"It was a river steamer coming in at dusk," he said, "just like the one I'd come in on. The nigger roustabouts on the decks were singing, and the stacks were puffing smoke and sparks, and her headlight was swinging back and forth across the levee. Little girls in the town were down at the dock to see if they'd be getting the new dolls and bonnets their folks back east promised to send out here. A cannon on the levee fires a salute. The steamer whistles an answer. You'd have thought it was one of those big ships from abroad coming into New York harbor. Two days later, the Blackfeet damn near got my scalp on the way overland to Alder Gulch."

These long years after, I am inclined to think I would have chosen the Missouri River route to Fort Benton. Still, I am not really sure about that. There must have been a kind of beauty about the plains crossing, the campfire at dusk, the music of the creaking harness, the first view of the snow-capped Rockies, the great, white-topped prairie schooners in the moonlight. For they, too, were ships.

Adolescent Interludes

1. The Business

It was a thoroughfare on which no lady who valued her reputation had ever been known to set foot, nor would she have done so even in 1918, two years after civic virtue's forces had put an end to open, licensed prostitution in Missoula. The girls were gone from the one-story, red-brick "cribs" that lined the farther end of West Front Street. The honky-tonks where pianos had jangled and the customers had fought, caroused and chosen their favorite ladies at leisure were dark and silent.

Still, a vaguely inviting air of sin hovered over West Front Street, although it certainly was not in my mind that morning. I was too preoccupied with another kind of commerce.

This was my thirteenth birthday, and my birthday present —the new, glittering, maroon bicycle—was not only a thing of beauty but a potential business asset. Until now, as the *Missoulian*'s newsboy responsible for delivering seventy newspapers daily on the South Side between 6:00 A.M. and 7:30, I had traveled afoot. The bicycle opened new vistas, a larger and more profitable territory. If I could find new subscribers, I could deliver half again as many papers on this splendid steed (I would be a Pony Express rider, St. Joe, Missouri to the Pacific Coast), and still have time to breakfast and get to school.

My regular round completed on this August morning—it

was a month until the new school term, but I was planning ahead—I turned down West Front Street in search of an expanded clientele.

A two-story building that somehow looked like a residence, even on this street of small restaurants and shops, seemed worth a try. It could not have been later than seven o'clock, but through the half-drawn curtain I could see someone moving about. Black leather subscription book open to a blank page, pencil in hand, I rang the bell. Almost at once a woman opened the door and said, "Well?"

She listened without speaking while I explained my mission, gazing at her as I talked, trying to size her up, businessman fashion: thirty-five or forty, I guessed, competent-looking, reddish hair combed tight, a plain gray dress, almost severe. Here was a new subscriber, all right, and, yes, she finally said, "I'll take your paper."

I prepared to enter the new subscriber's name in the black leather book. I was feeling very professional.

"What's the name?" I asked.

"Bonnie," she said.

"What's the last name?"

"The hell with the last name," she said.

Within my limited experience it was my impression that men usually were profane for no reason but women only when they were angry. This one was not angry. Suddenly she was smiling at me, a clear, direct smile unlike the patronizing smirk of most adults.

She said, "You'll leave that paper here on the steps every morning, and if it's raining or snowing ring the bell and someone—me—will come and get it." She spoke, I observed with approval, like someone used to authority. I liked that. It was professional. "If you leave the paper out here to get soaked, you'll lose a customer and maybe get your tail kicked, too."

But she was still smiling as she said this, and I could see that she didn't mean all of it.

As fall moved into winter, it was often snowing or raining.

The first time I rang the bell she came to the door herself.

"You'll come into the kitchen and have some cocoa. You look cold," she said. It was not an order, or even an invitation. It was a statement.

I followed her through a parlor that had a dry, sweet smell about it. There were deep chairs, a pink-shaded lamp, starched white curtains, all very neat.

"You've got a nice house," I said. I reflected also that it was a pretty big place for one person, but of course that was no concern of mine.

She laughed, I couldn't see why, and went on ahead into a kitchen. The hot cocoa was ready, as if she had foreseen that I would need it. As I gulped it she gave me that direct, clear look.

"I've got an idea you're worried about something," she said, although I don't remember that I was. "Is it money? Most people worry about money."

She reached across the kitchen table and picked up my subscription book. She leafed through its pages, each containing the name of a subscriber, showing where he lived and whether or not he had paid to date. Most of them had not. She paused over the names of two or three leading citizens.

"Imagine those guys not paying on time," she said.

"They just forget," I said. "I always get it sooner or later."

"Listen," she said. "You got to be businesslike, or they don't respect you. Forget that sooner-or-later stuff."

Before I could stop her, but I didn't really try to, she was taking all the slips out of the book and rearranging them on the kitchen table.

"This'll give you a faster route," she said. "Look, cut over from Second Street to Gerald Avenue and back to Third Street. . . . Maybe fifteen minutes faster, so you can take your time eating breakfast when you're through. Is your mother a good cook?"

My mother was a wonderful cook, I said.

"Fine," said Bonnie. "If you work, you got to stay in shape."

I heard footsteps upstairs and was momentarily startled, but the footsteps were none of my concern, either.

"Beat it," she said. "Are you going to make 'em pay on time?"

"Yes," I said, because I could see that here was a very smart woman who might easily have become some sort of executive.

There was the morning a few weeks later when one of our conversations over the hot cocoa was interrupted. The footsteps from above came down the stairs, and there was a girl standing in the doorway, in a loose-fitting kimono that somehow embarrassed me. Her blonde hair was uncombed and her cheeks oddly red. A daughter? I judged that she was angry. I was right.

"That's a fine lot of bastards we got comin' in here these days," she snarled in a tone that bit. "That last one took a ten right off the top of the bureau."

"Shut up! Get out of here!" Bonnie yelled at her. I jumped and spilled the cup of cocoa. This was Bonnie as I had never seen or heard her. The girl went away sullenly. When I turned to look at Bonnie, she was herself again. Her eyes were kind, and so was her voice, as she said, "I think maybe I won't be taking the paper any more. Some day you'll see why."

After that, when we met on the street, she would smile and say, "Everything all right? They paying you? You staying healthy?"

"Yes, Bonnie," I would say, pleased that she, an adult, had asked me, a boy scarcely in his teens, to call her by her first name, because it meant that we were friends.

Presently she was gone from Missoula, and I never saw her again, although I learned years later that she had married a

Colorado millionaire lumberman. He was a lucky man, I thought. I still think so.

2. Unscheduled Stop

High on the south wall of Hell Gate Canyon, through which Blackfoot and Flathead Indians once had passed on war raids and the Northern Pacific and Chicago, Milwaukee and St. Paul railroad tracks now ran on opposite sides of the Missoula River, a couple of thirteen-year-old friends looked out upon the world and found it good. They were myself and Evan Reynolds, a thin, tall, red-haired, pale-faced boy with a Welsh temper and an artist's eye, son of a burly old-school sheriff in Central Montana who was now a Special Agent for the Northern Pacific in Missoula.

My friend and I, on this summer afternoon, had buried a small tin box, containing twenty-five pennies, a sheaf of United Cigar coupons and a packet of cigarette card pictures of baseball players, and had drawn a map, deriving from the one in *Treasure Island*, indicating how this treasure trove could be located by our heirs a century hence.

That game over and an oath of secrecy sworn, we fell to tossing stones down the long slide of loose shale rock that descended steeply to the C. M. & St. P. tracks beside the river. Launched on a discussion of Kid Curry's holdup of a Great Northern train a few years before in Northeastern Montana, we paused to note that the shale slide was on the move. Soon it was building into a small landslide. Suddenly it was a noisy avalanche. The shale started larger rocks into motion. Together the shale and rocks were piling up on the tracks.

"Look," said Evan, in a voice that seemed to come from a far distance. He was pointing toward the eastern end of Hell Gate. In utter silence the electrically powered *Olympian*, the C. M. & St. P.'s crack passenger train, Chicago to Portland, was snaking its way through the canyon. It was now a mile or so away from the rocky pile-up on the tracks. It did not appear to be slowing down.

God Almighty, let him see it! I thought. It was the most earnest prayer I had ever sent up from below. (My mother, a Unitarian, had small regard for the invocation of divine intervention.) By "him" I meant the engineer. He did see it. The long, beautiful orange train eased to a stop, fifty yards short of disaster. The engineer and the chief conductor climbed down and surveyed the mess. They gazed up, with a baleful suspicion, at the side of the canyon where two boys envisaging a term in the state reform school hid behind a boulder. The train crew appeared with shovels and toiled for twenty minutes in the sun. The *Olympian* moved on to its station stop a mile away in Missoula while the two boys went on up the side of the canyon, over the top of Mt. Sentinel, and home by a long, roundabout route.

The next day's *Missoulian* stated that for the first time in a dozen years the C. M. & St. P.'s great train had been delayed for a reason other than snow.

The potential criminals, fully recovered, swore a second oath of secrecy. Along with a sense of relief, they felt a certain pride.

"Kid Curry couldn't have stopped a train better," said Evan.

There I was again, back in the Old West. The day's excitement, I am sorry to have to say, lingered longer than any reflections I may have had on the efficacy of prayer.

3. Harvest Rodeo

Those were the golden September times, the last week end of that month, when it came time to head down the Bitter Root Valley and over the Continental Divide to the town of

Wisdom and its annual Harvest Rodeo. It was by way of
being a ritual—Dougal McCormick pulling up before our
house in his chocolate-colored Winton with a hood half
again as long as the ordinary car's; Dougal, brother to our
local Congressman (when the Republicans won), Washington J. McCormick, an urbane spellbinder and Dougal's opposite in personality, appearance and way of life.

Dougal, rumor had it, was an unofficial "fixer" for the
Anaconda Copper Mining Company, which found its way
into every corner of Montana's financial, legislative and social
life; a political handyman for The Company and for his
brother; a talker on street corners, a quiet visitor to the Flathead Indian Reservation when the Indians became eligible to
vote. If Dougal, a paunchy bachelor comfortable in unkempt
clothes, had any means of support, they were not visible.

Into the trunk of the Winton went a couple of suitcases
while my father settled himself in the front seat, beside Dougal, and my friend Evan and I lolled in the back one. My
father's cigar smoke drifted back to us with a rich air of holi-
day well-being, and his and Dougal's talk—political gossip,
mostly—in provocative snatches. Burton K. Wheeler would
be running for the Senate this year, "Bolshevik Burt," and
what were the chances of beating him? Alas, the chances were
slim. The sages in the front seat nodded their heads sadly. Mr.
Wheeler had the blessing of our revered United States Senator Thomas J. Walsh, soon to become famous as the bulldog
of the Teapot Dome investigation. The talk ran on, while
Evan and I chattered in the back seat and reckoned there was
no pleasure like whirling down the Bitter Root in an open car
on an autumn afternoon, past snow-topped Mount Lolo, past
Marcus Daly's great estate at Hamilton with its porticoed
house and vestiges of the private racetrack where his great
thoroughbreds, Tammany, Hamburg, Ogden and the rest,
had trained; on down to the end of the valley where it nar-
rows and the road turns east into the hills leading to the Divide. There was dinner at Medicine Hot Springs, rainbow

trout fresh from the stream, and then Dougal was taking the Winton up the steep, twisting road toward the summit of the Divide, guiding it around the turns as if it were a child's toy, never once blowing the horn.

"You'll have a grand smash-up some day if you aren't careful," my father would say.

"Have I ever had an accident?" Dougal would say, never having dented so much as a fender.

The Winton surged across the Divide and started down the long corridorlike highway lined with slender pines. The ignition would be off, now, to cool the engine heated by the steep upward climb. Our way was a ghostly, silent rush past the Big Hole Battlefield where Chief Joseph and his Nez Percés had held their own against Colonel John Gibbon and the United States Army. A Nez Percé's war cry, or the firing of a carbine, would have been no great surprise just now.

And then, suddenly, we could see the lights of Wisdom, some ten miles away, and under a bearskin robe in the back seat Evan and I shivered with a certain happy anticipation as well as the night air's chill. The Harvest Rodeo was Wisdom's big show, when the days were sunny and clear for the doings in the little arena, and the nights brisk and noisy, and everybody felt fine. Things would be getting under way at about this hour, people tramping up and down the boardwalks past the false-front stores, talking and laughing and dropping in here and there for a drink at places that seemed not to have heard of the Prohibition Amendment. Dougal's car wheeled smartly down onto the floor of the Big Hole Valley, and there we were. He and my father would be politicking around and visiting with old friends from Butte and Helena. Evan and I would be on our own. When we were ready to sleep, we would climb onto a haystack under the bearskin robe and the light of the full moon.

"Here's a little entertainment fund," said my father, handing me five silver dollars. "Try to keep out of trouble."

This was the nearest to cattle country that our part of

Western Montana knew. Cowboys and cowgirls, local and visiting, walked the streets, their spurs rasping on the boardwalks. Their rolling gait was that of people who spent more time in the saddle than out of it. They were talking about tomorrow's rodeo program, and the prize money that wasn't much by big-time rodeo standards, but this didn't matter here. This was like a small-town picnic where neighbors compete and have something to talk about over the winter.

This evening they were talking mostly about a boy named Ad Jackson, who could stay aboard a bronc so long without pulling leather that in a year or so he might be ready for the major circuit, Cody and Pendleton. Cowpokes rode through Wisdom's single, dusty street, side by side with the Pierce-Arrows of Butte's copper-rich, flashily dressed first families. Dice were rolling and cards were slapping in a makeshift gambling spot, and, weighed down by those five silver dollars, I was briefly tempted. But only briefly. This was going to be a long evening, and five dollars had to go quite a distance.

The crowd was drifting toward a big dance hall where a ring had been set up for a six-round exhibition between Dixie La Hood, the pride of Butte and a potential contender for the bantamweight title, and a Big Hole Valley boy with modest aspirations. The Valley boy was more strenuous with a wild right hand than the code of boxing exhibitions calls for, but Dixie only smiled and let him off easily. Everybody was in excellent spirits this night. White moonshine whiskey was disappearing from tilted bottles at an astonishing rate after the ring was taken down and the dancing started, but nobody got ugly, though freshly concocted Montana moonshine had a reputation for meanness. The dance tickets were three for twenty-five cents, and before I knew it I had danced away most of my five dollars and was in love with a blonde ranch girl of my own age—sixteen—whose mother put an end to this romance shortly after midnight.

"You come home now, Emma Lou," said her mother. "A

girl that's riding the barrel race tomorrow needs her sleep."

An acute sense of inferiority momentarily crushed me. Dancing with a latter-day Pony Express Rider, maybe a female Buffalo Bill, *I* had been trying to impress *her*. Inferiority gave way to fatigue. The moon floated high and cold over the haystack where Evan and I slept the rest of the night away under Dougal's bearskin robe. The sun rose red and near. On Main Street we met Dougal and my father for a breakfast of country sausage and fried eggs, double orders of each. This was the happy life, all right, and now the excitement was building toward the afternoon's program in the little arena that was packed by one o'clock.

On the bare benches, in the sun's glare, we sat while a trumpet, a saxophone and a drum from last night's dance ran through assorted medleys, winding up with a rendition of the official State anthem ("M-O-N-T-A-N-A, Montana, I Love You") and then the master of ceremonies, on a prancing roan, was announcing the Ladies' Barrel Race.

There was my blonde heroine, Emma Lou, on a sure-footed cow pony that cut just outside three barrels, arranged in a triangle, with a time-saving neatness that brought her back to the starting line in first place. The crowd's cheers rang with hometown affection, and the show went on, the calf roping, bulldogging, trick roping. The shadows were growing a little longer as the show came to its climax, the bronc riding that couldn't have been for more than a fifty-dollar prize but in this place might as well have been for a national championship.

"Ad Jackson on Skybolt!" the announcer hollered through a megaphone, and out of the chute came a tow-headed boy of perhaps eighteen on a piebald that reared, bucked, plunged— and hadn't thrown him when the whistle blew. He was still in competition for the third, and final, go-around, his rivals a couple of seasoned bronc riders from Idaho, over beyond the Bitter Root Mountains. Now, for the first time during the long afternoon, the crowd fell silent.

"Ad Jackson on Cactus!" the announcer called out, and he sounded a little subdued, as if vaguely apprehensive, because this was the meanest bronc of the day, a savage bent on the removal of the rider whose weight on its back it clearly regarded as an intolerable degradation.

Cactus pawed for the sky, came down, and veered abruptly toward the arena's board fence. In a single voice of despair the crowd yelled, "Look out, Ad!" It was too late for Ad to look out or to do anything else. The bronc hit the fence, and when it bounced away, still plunging, Ad was on the ground beside the fence, his right leg twisted at a sickening angle, blood masking his face. In a swoop like a darting shadow in the fading sunlight, Emma Lou was on her knees beside him.

"First cousin," said a woman in the row behind us. "Raised up together."

Suddenly the day was over. Maybe the boy would die, maybe he wouldn't, but there could be no more of this Harvest Rodeo. Its gala air drained away with the splashes of blood sliding down the board fence and seeping into the ground even after Ad had been carried off.

The regal Pierce-Arrows moved out across the prairie toward Butte, the Winton toward Missoula. For a long time no one in our car spoke, until the usually jocular Dougal said, in a strained voice, "I reckon the boy won't ever ride again." Nor did he, at least in a rodeo. But he did marry his cousin Emma Lou, several years later, and with her had a good life, a number of children, a ranch that prospered.

4. Pioneer's Funeral

"Try to remember as much of this as you can," my father said. We were boarding a train for Deer Lodge, some eighty miles to the east, where Granville Stuart's funeral was to be held that day—Granville Stuart, who with his brother James in 1858 made the first gold discovery in what later was to be named Montana; who, with James, had operated a general merchandise store in Alder Gulch and had been a Vigilante; who had been a king of the Central Montana cattle country and fought the cattle-rustling gangs to a finish, married an Indian wife and did not discard her when civilization moved in, had a passion for good books and on his ranch near Gilt Edge maintained a library of three thousand of them, and wrote a posthumously published book of memoirs that remains an invaluable record of the Northwest frontier.

"Just possibly the greatest of all Montana pioneers," my father said.

Greater than Marcus Daly, Colonel Sanders and the rest?

"I said 'just possibly,'" my father said.

Granville Stuart had occasionally joined the circle of old men whom I had heard reminiscing on summer afternoons—in fact, he was the oldest of them, or, anyhow, he was the one who had been here longest, ever since 1857. His white mane was patriarchal, his manner courtly and self-assured, as became one who knew his way around Shakespeare as well as the Rockies. In the Sun River country up toward the border in the 1880's, when marauding Blackfeet, Gros Ventres and Assiniboines still roamed, his DHS Ranch was an empire in itself. The great buffalo herds were gone by this time, wiped out by calculated policy to reduce the Indians to dependence on the United States Government. The homesteaders had not arrived. The range was open. They were giants of the plains, those early cattlemen—Nelson Story, the first of them, who trailed a herd of one thousand longhorns from Texas to Montana in 1866, and Conrad Kohrs, and Granville Stuart. The Northern Pacific Railroad had finally pushed west into Montana. The way was direct to the rich eastern market for beef. A man could be a tycoon in no great while with a small stake, and with some luck from the weather and protection against Indians and wolves, each seeking a substitute for the vanished buffalo meat. Grass was plentiful and so, presently, were white outlaws—the wolfers, lowest and foulest-smelling of all western characters, who trapped and poisoned wolves to get the cash bounty on their hides, and the buffalo hunters who merged in gangs to steal horses and rustle cattle. Holed up in the wild brakes of the Missouri River, downstream from Fort Benton, they raided skillfully and successfully. Here was Alder Gulch's lawlessness once more, and again the victims went into action—"Stuart's Stranglers," their unofficial name was, not to be used in Mr. Stuart's presence; a "Vigilance Committee," in Mr. Stuart's more polite term. Before 1884's summer ended, between twenty and seventy-five outlaws were hanged or otherwise destroyed—no one ever made a specific count. In any case, the rustlers were gone. And gone from the range, after the terrible winter of 1886-87 that decimated Montana's livestock, was Granville Stuart.

"A business that had been fascinating," said Mr. Stuart, who wrote and spoke precisely, "suddenly became distasteful. I never wanted to own again an animal that I could not feed and shelter."

His Shoshone wife dead after a quarter century of marriage during which she bore him nine children, he served four years as American Minister to Uruguay and Paraguay and came home to enjoy the admiration and respect of his fellow Montanans. An inch or so over six feet, gaunt and handsome, the Virginia-born book-lover naturally dominated the annual conventions of the Society of Montana Pioneers, which he founded. . . . Now the dean was dead, and in Deer Lodge the clan was gathering. At the graveside stood old General Charles Warren, Indian fighter, and "Fat Jack" Jones, Butte's renowned hack driver for Presidents, mining magnates and madams. Tears shone in old, dim eyes. Hands that had swung lariats and pulled guns in split-second, life-and-death battle trembled in the October sunshine. I saw no tears, however, in the ice-blue eyes of a small, ferret-faced man in an expensive-looking overcoat with a fur neckpiece. He wore a gleaming silk hat. His expression was unchanging.

"Who is that?" I whispered.

"That is William Andrews Clark," my father replied, with a look of what Mr. Stuart might have called "distaste."

XII

Titans

A MAJOR PROBLEM in writing or talking about early-day Montana, my father used to say, was that you could state the exact truth and yet no outsider—no Easterner, especially—would be likely to believe you. Most storytellers, he added, feel themselves obliged to "color" and "heighten," but in the case of Montana, as of the Old West in general, they could make themselves credible only if they toned down the reality. Consider, he would offer by way of example, the eventually related stories of William Andrews Clark, Marcus Daly and F. Augustus Heinze.

Hearing from him and from others what they knew at first hand about those men, and in later years reading what others had written about them, I realized what my father meant. Who indeed would easily believe the sagas of a penny-pinching trader from Pennsylvania who found his way across the country in the 1860's, assembled a fortune of two hundred million dollars, bought his way into the United States Senate, built a one-hundred-room mansion at Fifth Avenue and Seventy-seventh Street? Of a warm-hearted Irishman who struck it rich in Butte, seemed to prefer race horses and old friendships to money but strangely sold his corporate child, the Anaconda Company, and with it his State, to the colonial-minded Standard Oil? Of the polished bandit-genius who arrived in Butte at the age of twenty as a five-dollar-a-day mining surveyor and left it, seventeen years later, with ten and one-half million dollars obtained under duress from his Standard Oil enemies?

Clark, Daly, Heinze—their names rang throughout Montana, and still ring, their heritage of good and evil still enduring there. They created and they corrupted. Of the three, Daly and Heinze had died less than twenty years before my Montana life began. But William Andrews Clark remained a living, if chilly, presence.

What was behind that pale, utterly expressionless face, with its bushy (once reddish) whiskers, its icy eyes? A passion for money and power, his life story said: a fixed, relentless greed. The oldest old-timers, who had known him as a trader in Bannack, said so. There never was such a man, they declared, for making two dollars appear where only one had been visible before. Oh, yes, he was a smart one, that little Scotch-Irish Presbyterian. Back East, he had studied law and taught school. Some said he had been briefly in the Confederate Army, but no official record of his service ever was located. If he did take part in the Civil War, was he a deserter? Possibly. A Confederate private soldier's chances for money-making were slim. He was a reader, though. In the pack on his back when he came up to Bannack from Colorado in 1863 were Robert Burns' *Poems* and *Parsons on Contracts*, and a geology textbook. When he spoke, which in those days was seldom, it was in a thin, high voice. He cultivated no friends for friendship's sake. Discovering that the best mining claims along Bannack's Grasshopper Creek were taken up, he turned to merchandising. He dealt in the lumber necessary for placer miners' sluice boxes. He found a pair of elk antlers and sold them for ten dollars to the Bannack saloon keeper, Cyrus Skinner, a road agent later hanged by the Vigilantes. For two dollars a day he cut and hauled firewood. Investing in a team and wagon, he made the eight-hundred-mile round trip in winter to Salt Lake and returned with a profitable store of goods, including frozen eggs to be sold at three dollars a dozen to egg-hungry Bannack. On a visit to his family in Iowa, he characteristically bought and sold a few barrels of pork to pay his vacation expenses. Only a few years after he arrived penniless in Bannack, he was a well-to-do merchant and banker in Deer Lodge and was contemplating the possibilities of picking up mining properties in Butte. Again characteristically, he prepared himself for this new enterprise with a course in minerology at the Columbia School of Mines in New York, returned and bought several Butte silver mines, tricked a miner out of an ore-crushing mill that he, the new tycoon, needed, and was on his way to those millions of which he never had enough. William Andrews Clark had his critics, but none ever accused him of lazily overlooking a dime or a million.

There was every reason, the old-timers used to say, why William Andrews Clark and Marcus Daly should come to hate each other. It would be hard to picture two men more unlike, save for the Irish blood in each. But even in their Irishness they differed. Marcus Daly, from Tommy Cruse's County Cavan, laughed and talked, took long chances on a horse or a mine, and loved his friends. No one ever saw William Andrews Clark, millionaire, sitting in old clothes on a curbstone chatting with cronies of other years. He could not have done it. But Marcus Daly, millionaire, enjoyed nothing more than such a conversation, unless it was the sight of one of his horses coming in at 40-to-1. Over a cheerful glass with a comrade from his Comstock Lode days who might be down on his luck, Marcus Daly would promise a percentage of the next mining deal of his that worked out—and, the Daly word being the Daly bond, that old comrade would presently be rich. Montana fortunes that still exist were born that way, although the latter-day beneficiaries do not always choose to acknowledge it.

Marcus Daly, the stocky, hearty man, an Irish emigrant selling newspapers on the streets of New York at fifteen, a

California-Nevada argonaut by way of a steerage passage and the Isthmus of Panama, came to Butte in 1876 as representative of a Salt Lake City mining investment firm. For his employers he bought a silver mine, retaining a one-third interest for himself. He sold his one-third interest and bought another silver mine, the Anaconda, but, lacking capital to develop it, went outside the State to find the capital to finance it—a foreshadowing of Montana's economic dependence on sources other than its own. Was Daly, the shrewd, practical miner who never had to take a mineralogy course, entirely surprised when his Anaconda mine revealed an incredible seam of copper, the first real hint of the deposit that was to make Butte The Richest Hill on Earth, launch a war of millionaires, and throw Montana into turmoil?

Whether or not he was surprised, he kept his secret, closing down his mine and letting it be understood that it was worthless, the better to buy up adjoining land and claims. He could not buy it all, and soon he had a fellow copper king and enemy in the person of William Andrews Clark, but Marcus Daly was the man Butte loved. Was there ever such a one, Butte asked, so quick with a smile, a handshake, a pay raise, or a hundred dollars or five thousand dollars passed along to a needy friend so quietly that it had no air of charity? And the way the man spent his money—there was a true Irishman for you. He did not merely build a big house. He created an estate over west in the Bitter Root Valley, with stables and a covered running track with connecting water pipes and electric light wires, the home of such memorable thoroughbreds and stake race champions as Tammany, Ogden, Hamburg, Inverness. Who but Marcus Daly would create a whole city, Anaconda, site of the smelter for his ever-increasing copper ore? Knowing Marcus Daly, Butte was not startled when it heard how, as he and his engineers stood on a hill planning the new town's design, a cow strolled across the valley. "Main Street," said Mr. Daly, "will run north and south straight through that cow." Was there a finer hotel in all Montana than Mr. Daly's Montana Hotel, at Main Street and Park Avenue, Anaconda, with a mosaic of his great horse, Tammany, inlaid on the parquet floor? Was there a better newspaper in the United States, for a city of its size, than Mr. Daly's Anaconda *Standard*, edited by the scholarly John Durstin, imported by Mr. Daly from the Syracuse *Standard*, way back in New York State?

Marcus Daly, his admirers could state convincingly, was incomparable.

All this could have been viewed only with dismay by William Andrews Clark, whom many feared, whom no one loved. The Daly name and fame were rivaling his own. The Clark vanity responded. Perhaps the answer lay, he must have decided, in politics. In the summer of 1888 he won the Democratic nomination as Territorial delegate to Congress, in Democratic Montana an all but certain prelude to final victory in November. But Clark was defeated then by a Republican unknown whose votes came from Democratic strongholds controlled by Daly. Shouts of a double-cross arose from Clark quarters. The war was on, although the two antagonists arranged a truce during the Montana Constitutional Convention of 1889 which obligingly provided for a minimum of taxation on the net profits of mining operations—a curse that would bedevil Montana well into the following century.

Those were the high days, the old-timers would tell you, when the sky above was Butte's limit in one direction, and the deep, intricately connected and winding tunnels and shafts were its limit in another. On Butte's arid, sloping surface there were few limits for any sort of behavior at all.

Three thousand feet and more down in The Richest Hill on Earth, Daly's Irish miners fought Clark's Cornish miners with picks, axes and live steam. Up above, Daly's Anaconda *Standard* fought Clark's Butte *Miner*. Union Veterans battled with Confederate veterans. With skilled labor earning as much as six dollars a day, the camp's payroll (Butte always was as much mining camp as city) rose to five hundred thousand dollars a month. The money stayed there, and made the rounds—the predatory East had not yet captured it. At John McGuire's Theater, Sarah Bernhardt, Minnie Maddern Fiske and John Drew appealed to representatives of the city's superior taste. The same cultured patrons were also likely to drop in later at the Casino and the Comique to watch the girls dance on tables while other girls "rustled the boxes" in balconies to which clients had access by private stairways, and drinks were passed through a slide in a door lest the occupants be interrupted in what might have been called shameful practices if Butte had worried much about shame. In the red light district were the drabs in the shoddy "cribs," and the fancy, pretty ladies in Lou Harpell's elegant parlor house, reputed to challenge comparison with the Everleigh Sisters' gilded temple of sin in Chicago. When Daly's mighty stake horse, Montana, took the Suburban at 40-to-1, roulette wheels spun through the night and Madam Harpwell's sirens never had more generous customers. J. P. Morgan came to town, was hit by a tomato while riding through Butte's Dublin Gulch, and was advised by "Fat Jack" Jones, the renowned and phenomenally thin hack driver, not to leave the carriage and attempt to retaliate unless he chose to risk being torn to pieces by Dublin Gulch's wild Irish. And Marcus Daly and William Andrews Clark were warming up for further rounds in a war that would end only with the death of one of them.

When, in 1892, Montanans failed to register a majority vote for one city over another as the new State's capital, they held a run-off election in 1894 to choose between the two leading contenders: Daly's town, Anaconda, and Helena, the town in which Clark was, anyhow, least disliked. Clark liquor went into the logging camps and won votes. Daly distributed not only liquor but cigars labeled Anaconda-for-the-Capital. The cigars were denounced in Clark's *Miner* as made by scab labor. A Daly partisan yelling "Hurray for Anaconda!" in Helena's Last Chance Gulch was jailed. Daly, characteristically, arranged a writ of habeas corpus and a money-making mining lease for him. Clark, and Helena, won the election, nor was the common sense of the electorate to be condemned. Montana loved Marcus Daly, but good men not to be bought by free liquor and cigars had reasonable doubts about selecting as the State's capital a city dominated by one man and his corporation. Each faction had spent about a million dollars in a contest involving only fifty thousand voters. Montanans were learning early the joys of riding on a political gravy train.

But the climactic battles were still to come. In 1898 William Andrews Clark, cherishing a long-held dream of representing Montana in the United States Senate, set out in earnest to insure his arrival there. Marcus Daly, it could be assumed, would fight him with all the Daly energy and dollars. By this time, however, Clark had an imposing ally, Frederick Augustus Heinze.

Now there was a man like no other that Montana ever knew, said the old-timers: a personal charmer, a public orator of hypnotic eloquence, a fighter, a freebooter. A most elegant freebooter, to be sure, who has his admirers in Montana to this day, almost sixty years after he said good-bye to it.

He was scarcely out of his teens when he arrived there in 1889, an Irish-German, Brooklyn-born lad, educated at the Columbia School of Mines, content to work at a minute salary for the Boston and Montana Mining Company while he studied Butte's underground labyrinth and plotted his future field of operations. Well before silver crashed in 1893, he knew that copper was to be the great Montana bonanza, greater than gold at its most glittering. But first he needed capital and a working knowledge of financial manipulation. He returned to New York to study Wall Street as a staff member of the *Engineering and Mining Journal*. He took a course in metallurgy at a German university. At a time that could not have been more opportune, he inherited fifty thousand dollars. He went back to Butte not yet ready for full-scale battle with the titans but getting steadily closer, and leased two unpromising mines that he promptly turned into money-makers. He built a smelter to process the ores from his own and other, independently owned mines. Still short of the means with which to encounter Clark and Daly on equal terms, he moved across the border into British Columbia, built a smelter, acquired a newspaper, launched a noisy campaign against the Canadian Pacific Railway, threatened to build a rival railroad, and frightened the Canadian Pacific into paying him more than a million dollars to go away.

Back to the scarred, feverish mining camp known as Butte went F. Augustus Heinze, now armed for war.

Cosmopolitan as it was, Butte never had seen anyone quite like this one, the handsome, well-groomed, well-mannered, widely traveled bachelor, still in his twenties, who entertained with a princely, winning air, and was admired by men and women alike. He was the new generation, a suave bandit more appealing to the populace than that cool, self-righteous man of avarice, William Andrews Clark. "Fritz" Heinze was a gambler, if a man so sure of what he was doing could be called a gambler. Montana cherished gamblers, and, yes, bandits too, if they had style.

The Heinze style flashed at once upon his return from Canada to Butte. To the rage of the Boston and Montana Mining Company that once had employed him, Heinze tore into that company's rich, adjoining ore, his raid staged under the provisions of the Apex Law whereby the owner of property in which a vein of ore reached its apex on the surface could follow that vein downward and laterally into the property of another. Such an apex had appeared on the surface of the Rarus, a mine Heinze had bought at a bargain price. He raided his neighbor, the Boston and Montana, to which he had casually offered two hundred and fifty thousand dollars for ore that proved to be worth twenty million. The victim petitioned for an injunction against the Heinze depredations. Heinze was ready for that, too. On the bench of the District Court, thanks to the political support of Heinze, sat one William Clancy, a tobacco-spitting barfly who came out of his non-judicial snooze long enough at any hour of day or night to render any decision requested by his sponsor. Whoever sued Heinze was confronted by multiple suits in return. While the cases appealed from the wayward judgments of Judge Clancy awaited the attention of the State Supreme Court, Heinze went on extracting ore from the claims surrounding his. It was almost too easy.

Presently he was faced with a more formidable enemy. Marcus Daly secretly, perhaps shamefacedly, sold his Anaconda Company to the Standard Oil Company, on whose behalf Standard Oil's Henry H. Rogers arrived in Montana to shape the Amalgamated Copper Company. But before Montana took a ringside seat at the one-sided spectacle of F. Augustus Heinze versus the Rockefeller millions, it watched one more struggle between those old, incessantly bitter enemies, Marcus Daly and William Andrews Clark.

In the Montana of my boyhood they were still talking about it, that session of the Legislature which met in January, 1899, to elect a United States Senator. Daly himself was without personal political ambition. He was determined only that Clark should not go to Washington, no matter how much the crafty little man was prepared to spend in bribes. From the far corners of the State, then, came the hungry solons, rubbing their receptive hands in anticipation of the impending fiesta. Had not one of Clark's sons, acting as his father's campaign manager, said that "we'll send the old man either to the Senate or the poorhouse"? A candidate supported by Daly led in the early balloting. The price of a vote for Clark rose accordingly. It varied from day to day and was cited in the bars and hotel lobbies as if it were a stock market quotation, which in a sense it was. When an incredibly honest State Senator, having led the Clark pay-off men to believe that he and three other legislators were for sale, rose in the State Senate chamber and waved thirty thousand dollars in bills as proof of a Clark bribe attempt, the populace gasped—but more in excitement than indignation. Clark casually called it a Daly frame-up and went on to acquire the votes of forty-seven State Senators, enough to elect him, for a carefully recorded total of four hundred and thirty-one thousand dollars. The infuriated Daly took the battle to the United States Senate Committee on Privileges and Elections. Faced with certain rejection by that committee, Clark resigned the seat he had not yet held, and waited. There would be another day.

While he waited, he formed an alliance of convenience with the busy F. Augustus Heinze, based on the enmity they shared for Marcus Daly and, now, Daly's monstrous new associate, Standard Oil-Amalgamated Copper. The Heinze-Clark alliance was sound. For reasons still not entirely clear, the most beloved of Montanans, Daly, had sold his Anaconda properties to Standard Oil for thirty-nine million dollars. Why? His motive could scarcely have been greed. He never had cared for money for its own sake. Was he merely weary after a strenuous life? Had he a premonition of his impending death? Montanans, too, must have had a premonition—of the Wall Street exploitation to come, of the draining away toward the East of so much of the State's resources. Marcus Daly was suddenly no longer so much beloved. Nothing could have worried Standard Oil-Amalgamated Copper less. Floating a watered-stock issue of seventy-five million dollars, it paid Daly his thirty-nine million without a cent of cost to itself, rigged the stock up and down with great profit to insiders and to the ruin of innocent investors. Big business had arrived in full force in Montana.

Perhaps to his own surprise, William Andrews Clark found

himself almost popular. The dashing Heinze, who could talk with miners and millionaires respectively in their own terms, already was a public favorite. When a new legislature was elected in 1900, which in turn would elect a new Senator that fall, the Clark-Heinze candidates won by majorities that made Clark's election a certainty. Montana political campaigns in my time struck me as being wild affairs, but the old-timers brushed them off with a derogatory shrug when they recalled that summer of 1900. "Clark's money, Heinze's gift of gab—how could you beat a combination like that?" The answer was, you could not. Heinze and Clark promising an eight-hour day to the Butte miners and challenging Amalgamated Copper to do the same. Heinze, in Missoula, shedding a crocodile tear for Marcus Daly and his "betrayal" by his new masters who had promised to let him manage Amalgamated Copper and then had double-crossed him. (There was little if any evidence to support this, but it captured the sympathy and votes of old Daly partisans.) Heinze and Clark rolling down the streets of Butte in a tally-ho while glee clubs, to the tune of "The Wearing of the Green," sang "We must down the kerosene, boys" and Heinze everywhere hammering away at a single, powerful theme: "Montana or Standard Oil—which do you choose?"

Returning from Europe to New York, the ailing Marcus Daly heard the shattering results of the November election that would send his old enemy to the United States Senate. To the New York hotel where Daly lay bed-ridden came a New York *Journal* reporter, Martin Hutchens, formerly of the Helena *Independent*, who had known and admired Daly.

"I'll dance on their graves yet, Martin," said Marcus Daly. But a week later he was dead, at fifty-eight.

His victory assured, Senator-elect William Andrews Clark promptly broke off his alliance with F. Augustus Heinze and entered upon a new one with Standard Oil-Amalgamated Copper. Henry H. Rogers, it was hinted, had suggested to the new Senator that while his election was relatively honest, by Montana standards, Standard Oil had enough friends in the United States Senate to reject him again if he failed to renounce Heinze. In any event, the Senator proved obliging, and, furthermore, sold some of his choicest Butte holdings to Amalgamated Copper-Standard Oil.

If Heinze was angry, he was too intelligent to be surprised by his late ally's defection. Nothing in the cold-blooded Clark nature promised any other course. Perhaps Heinze even welcomed the drama of the new, post-election situation: one man standing alone against America's richest man, John D. Rockefeller, and his chief agent in Montana, Henry H. Rogers, and Montana's richest man, William Andrews Clark. Whoever thought Heinze would quit was mistaken. His liquid assets were at a low point. What he had was nerve, property and the good will of Butte, which always did like gamblers. A new war was on.

Complacent over its acquisition of William Andrews Clark or, at least, his separation from Heinze, Amalgamated Copper might have briefly overlooked a Heinze victory far down on the winning Clark-Heinze ticket in November, 1900: the re-election to the bench of Heinze's amiable friend, Judge Clancy, and the election of another and no less agreeable judge, Edward Harney, both in Butte. Between them, while Amalgamated Copper swore and sweated, they gave Heinze everything he asked for in the kingdom for which he was fighting.

Side by side with Heinze's Rarus mine was the Boston and Montana Mining Company's Michael Davitt. Heinze looted it, and when the owner obtained a Federal Court injunction Heinze calmly created a new mining company, assigned to it his so-called rights under the Apex Law, and hoisted the Davitt's ore through the Rarus' shafts. He stole a million dollars of Michael Davitt copper, and for this was fined all of twenty thousand dollars, but even that could not be collected from the new, no-assets company he had established. One of his grateful judges then awarded him the rich Minnie Healey mine on the basis of a contract that was not signed and may not even have been a verbal one. With an offhand arrogance worthy of Henry Plummer in that bandit-sheriff's Alder Gulch heyday, Heinze declared that three of Amalgamated Copper's biggest mines "apexed" in one tiny claim he had staked out at a strategic point. In line with his usual practice, for every suit filed against him by his enemy, he filed two or three of his own. Standard Oil-Amalgamated Copper was growing fretful. The time had come to crush this nuisance for good.

Shortly after its representatives in court heard Judge Clancy drawl and spit his way through the decision presenting Heinze with the Minnie Healey, and further declaring Standard Oil-Amalgamated Copper a vile interloper in the life of Montana, the interloper took an extreme step. It closed down all its operations, from the mines of Butte—where its employees greatly outnumbered Heinze's—to the lumber camps of Western Montana. Twenty thousand men abruptly were out of work one October day in 1903 in a State where winter comes early. Not even Heinze, it seemed, could escape this pressure tactic by which he was made to appear a villain who had harassed Montana's largest employer beyond endurance.

His first response—that Standard Oil-Amalgamated Copper was deliberately lowering the value of its stock so that insiders could once more sell, buy and recoup—meant little to hungry men in Butte. Well, then, he would stand on the courthouse steps one afternoon and state his case and make his answer.

As late as the 1920's those who were there recalled that day as if it had been a week before. For all his charm and popularity, F. Augustus Heinze was taking a long chance. In that place where physical violence was taken for granted, it would have needed very little to send an angry crowd of ten thousand surging against him. He took that chance; "Fritz" Heinze of Brooklyn against the mighty Standard Oil and the miners who once had been his friends and now were cursing him. They listened coldly at first, but presently the Heinze magic was fully at work. As in the 1900 campaign, he pictured Standard Oil as an ogre darkening the sky:

"Rockefeller and Rogers have filched the oil wells of America, and in doing so they have trampled on every law, human and divine. They ruthlessly crushed every obstacle in their path. They wrecked railroad trains and put the torch to oil refineries owned by their competitors. They entered into a conspiracy with railroads, by which competitors were ruined and bankrupted. Sometimes they were caught in the act, but they bought the judges and saved themselves from prison stripes and punishment. The same Rockefeller and the same Rogers are seeking to control the executive, the judiciary, and the legislature of Montana."

He had them listening now, and slowly, under the spell of that resonant, familiar voice, he won them over.

"I defy any man among you to point to a single instance where I did one of you a wrong. These people are my enemies, fierce, bitter, implacable. But they are your enemies, too. If they crush me today, they will crush you tomorrow. They will cut your wages and raise the tariff in the company stores on every bite you eat and every rag you wear."

A delicately, astutely timed pause, and then two dozen words that Montanans would not forget:

"They will force you to dwell in Standard Oil houses while you live, and they will bury you in Standard Oil coffins when you die."

That did it, at least for the moment. The gun-bearing, bloodthirsty mob was his. Back to the saloons and the gulches went those whom he had held enthralled, for an hour and a half, by the force of will and voice. Did he mean what he said? The old-timers differed among themselves about this. But on that afternoon, they agreed, he was magnificent, if only as a performer.

His triumph was fleeting. Amalgamated Copper maintained its shut-down until the Governor of Montana consented to call a special session of the Legislature to pass a bill providing that any litigant could seek a change of venue if he believed a trial judge to be prejudiced. It wanted no more Judge Clancys. The bill made sense, but the climate of coercion in which it was passed set a precedent that would shackle Montana for half a century. No one could doubt now who was the boss. It was Amalgamated Copper, later to become the Anaconda Copper Mining Company. It controlled newspapers, legislatures, the judiciary, banks. By its demonstrated power to starve the people of the State into submission, it ruled that State over the occasional—the very occasional—resistance of rebels.

Examining the situation in which he now found himself, Heinze could have discerned only a second fiddler's role in the years to come in Butte. The enemy had all the percussion instruments. Still, he was not disarmed. He had, among other properties, the marvelous Minnie Healey mine, and the Rarus, and a smelter, and so on. In utmost secrecy he sold these and other assets to Standard Oil for ten and one-half million dollars in 1906, gave one typically large, elegant dinner, and set off in his private car for New York to engage his old foes on their home grounds. He had organized a new company, United Copper, set up a Stock Exchange firm, and bought a New York bank. But the old foes, smarting under the humiliation he had inflicted upon them in Butte, were lying in ambush for him. Within a year the Standard Oil forces, headed by the unforgetting Henry H. Rogers, smashed Heinze's United Copper Company, started a run on his bank that he could not meet, and ruined his Stock Exchange firm. What did it matter to them that this revenge was a major

factor in bringing on the Panic of 1907? Their upstart neme-
sis, Heinze, had been properly punished.

Tried and acquitted on charges of fraudulent banking
practice, the boy bandit came back to Butte. Montanans who
might have been expected to despise him for leaving them
at the mercy of Amalgamated Copper, and who had invested
and lost heavily in his United Copper, greeted him instead as
a hero. He was their "Fritz," who had made Standard Oil
wince as no other one man ever had. He had enough money
left to live comfortably, but otherwise he had little to live
for, and half a dozen years later he died. He was forty-four.
Montanans mourned. Montanans also thought it appropriate
that he expired of cirrhosis of the liver. A man has to lead a
hearty, convivial life to go out that way, they said.

With one of his great rivals dead, and the other all but
destroyed, William Andrews Clark had gone serenely on,
collecting dollars and coal mines, works of art and coffee
plantations, professing a sentimental interest in Montana but
selling more and more of his holdings there. After his ex-
pensively purchased and undistinguished term in the United
States Senate ended in 1907—a term in which he unsurpris-
ingly opposed President Theodore Roosevelt's program for
conservation of natural resources—Paris and New York saw
more of him than Butte did. When he died at eighty-six in
his gaudy New York castle, his fortune was variously esti-
mated at $150,000,000 to $250,000,000. No one was quite
sure. What Montana did become aware of was that he left
very little to the State in which he established that fortune or
to those who had served him for better or worse.

Among the latter was a grim-faced old Missoula lawyer
who had served as agent in transmitting much of the bribe
money for the future Senator in that fevered campaign in
Helena in 1898. My father and I, walking home from the
Missoulian office one night in 1925 not long after the Sen-

ator's will was made public, passed the old lawyer on the street. His gait was shuffling, his eyes glazed and bitter.

"You might be upset, too," said my father, "if you had walked in the shadow of the penitentiary wall as that man did for Senator Clark and then found yourself forgotten."

I remembered then the day of Granville Stuart's funeral, and my father's look of distaste as he glanced at the gleaming silk hat and the cold blue eyes of the last of the Montana titans.

XIII

My Father's Town

THIS WAS THE JOURNEY to which I had looked forward most of all, the one to the town where Martin Hutchens had been a happy young man so many years before. I was almost afraid to go. Perhaps, I thought, my father had romanticized it in affectionate memory. Even now, as we started east through Hell Gate Canyon in the old Hupmobile, he was saying that it is well for a person to like the town he lives in, and he was not running down Missoula, a beautiful place certainly, but——

But there could be only one Helena.

And to think, he went on, that Helena might not have happened at all if a mining party led by a Georgian named John Cowan, returning from an unproductive prospecting trip in Northeastern Montana, hadn't stopped to take one last chance with their pans and shovels on July 14, 1864, in a gulch winding down the east slope of the Continental Divide into the Valley of the Prickly Pear. If they found nothing, they swore, they would give it all up and start for home and civilization.

What they found was gold running one hundred fifty dollars to the pan in that gulch which became, and remains, Last Chance Gulch, Helena's main street. You can be sure that even if Cowan and his friends had missed it someone else would have made a strike there some day, but in that case would the town growing up around it have been the same kind of town? It seems unlikely. My father all but shuddered at the thought.

For a while Helena was a typically bustling gold camp, with its share of violence, sin and assorted forms of liveliness. But there always was an air about it, a tone, a quiet charm, unlike that of any other Montana town. Alone among the settlements that began with the glint of gold, it endured and flourished. Bannack, Virginia City, Confederate Gulch—they either died or faded. Get rich and get away, the slogan went in those places. But in Helena people settled down. When we got there in three or four hours, I would see why, my father said.

As long as he lived, he went on to say, he never would forget *his* first view of it. From a long way off, as the train rolled across the valley floor in the twilight of that November day in 1889, he could see it: the little town spread around the sides of a Rocky Mountain amphitheater, in the lee of the Continental Divide. The surrey, with the greenhorn from the East, toiled up Last Chance Gulch toward the office of the *Independent*. The Gulch was crowded with people already celebrating the Territory's transition to Statehood on the following day, November 8. They were noisily cheerful, and some of them called out greetings. The greenhorn knew for a certainty that he was going to like this place.

At the *Independent* he introduced himself and arranged for living quarters in a red brick boarding house hanging nervously (or so it seemed to him) on the edge of the Gulch, overlooking Edwards Street. The Wild West! He must see it for himself, as quickly as possible. He dropped in at one of Helena's finely ordered saloons, where the chandeliers winked brightly upon tolerably good copies of the Renaissance masters. With excitement running high in Helena this night, the saloon was not so well ordered as usual. An intoxicated drinker at the bar was arguing violently with the bartender. The customer, enraged at being invited to leave, pulled out a Colt six-gun, aimed it waveringly at the bartender, and fired. He missed. The bartender wrenched the gun away from him, turned it on its owner, and disabled him with a wound considerately inflicted only in the shoulder. My father glanced around the room. Not another person on his side of the bar, except the wounded man, was in sight. He looked again. The people who had lined the bar were on the floor or under tables. A distinguished-looking man in broadcloth arose, dusted himself off, and observed amiably to my father, "You come from places where these things don't happen, or you would have taken cover like everyone else."

My father agreed that this was so. They fell to talking, and presently my father was asking, with what he deemed a young man's proper deference to an older one, "And what part of the country do you come from, sir?"

The distinguished-looking man's affability vanished behind a chilly stare.

"No questions west of the Red River, young man. *No questions.*"

"So," my father concluded now, "I learned two extremely important lessons about the West before the end of my first day."

As the Hupmobile chugged up the west side of Priest Pass, nearing the crest of the Continental Divide, he was recalling the legend that the left wing of Confederate General Sterling Price's army—which never actually was mustered out—had moved to Montana and become the Democratic Party. Yet it was not entirely a legend, he said. Helena's society had a Southern tone, an easygoing warmth of manner. It was a busy town, but a sedate and cosmopolitan one, too. World-traveling mining engineers came here regularly. Somewhere, they figured, there had to be a mother lode for the millions in gold dust yielded by Last Chance and nearby gulches and gullies. English remittance men were on ranches for a hundred miles around, a world to themselves, younger sons of upper-class families, an occasional nobleman among them.

"God knows what trouble they'd got into at home so that

they were sent out here," my father said. "But out here they were all right. They were better than all right, when you got to know them."

Montanans, once they became accustomed to the English accent, took the visitors in stride. They could shoot and ride. No one who saw him, my father said, would ever forget a young remittance man who, on a bet, put a thin, small English saddle on an outlaw bronc and rode him into submission without once "pulling leather." They swam the Missouri River in winter. At the Christmas season they came into Helena determined to spend every dollar they brought with them. Even hard-drinking Helena seldom saw so much whiskey downed with so much poise, my father recalled, with admiration for a gift greatly respected in Last Chance Gulch. For two weeks those temporary guests drank, dined, discussed English politics, compared notes on misadventures from London to Hong Kong, recited Shakespeare, and returned, broke and contented, to the ranches where they were sitting out their exile. There was no surprise in Helena when the name of one or another of them turned up several years later in heroic light in the Boer War news.

What most Easterners never could seem to understand, my father said, was the cosmopolitanism of many points in the Far West at a time when a North Dakota farmer was still grubbing away in frontier hardship. If they stopped to think about San Francisco, he pointed out, they would realize how much of the sophistication of Helena, Butte and Denver came inland from the Pacific Coast to which it had made its way around Cape Horn or across the Isthmus of Panama: books and fashions, pianos and theater. . . . Now we were across the Divide and coasting down past Colonel Charles A. Broadwater's Broadwater Hotel and Natatorium, the marvel of the day when that merchant prince built it in 1888, a little seedy by the 1920's but a wonder still: a huge, rambling framework in more or less Moorish design, with stained glass windows and broad verandahs, and a hot water swimming pool a hundred yards long.

"We'll stop there on the way back," said my father, "so that you can say some day how you saw with your own eyes a solid Italian marble bathtub with a solid gold strip around the inside of it to mark the soap ring level."

Just now he was in a hurry. So was I.

Then I saw it, the broad valley floor off to the east, the shadows of drifting clouds racing across it, and, beyond, the blue haze of the Big Belt Mountains. Below us was the city, and for a dazzling moment—as so often before when coming for the first time to a Montana scene—I had the sensation of having been here before. There was the twin-spired cathedral, Tommy Cruse's church. At the head of the Gulch was Watch Tower Hill, with its bell tower where a warden stood ready in pioneer times to sound the alarm by striking a large iron triangle. A mile to the east of the Gulch, on a kind of plateau of its own, the copper-sheathed dome of the State Capitol shone dully. Everywhere were splashes of weathered red brick, the mansions of the early-day well-to-do. It came to me, then, the quality that set this town apart from other Montana towns. It looked *old*, as they—except for the crumbling ghost towns—did not. Old, but alive.

We glided down the long eastern slope of the Divide, into the head of the Gulch, and pulled up at the Placer Hotel. We dined leisurely and well. Then my father said, "We will take a walk."

It was one of those mid-summer evenings when, in the Rockies, the twilight runs past nine o'clock, the red of the sunset fading into an overhanging violet haze. We started up the Gulch, and at 108 Broadway stood outside the *Independent* building, but did not go in. Glancing at my father, I could guess why. A man of sentiment, he was averse to a too-open display of it. We went on into what had been Helena's lively Chinatown. On first venturing into this area, one midnight in 1889, young Martin Hutchens heard a woman's scream and saw a flight of pigtails around a corner. In the gutter lay a Chinese girl from one of the dingy "cribs" on the hillside. She was decapitated. The new reporter hurried back to his office, to be told that this was scarcely a news story because, among other reasons, the identity of the murderer could never conceivably be established.

At Water Street and the Gulch we stood before an empty building. My father said, "Ah Sam's opium den." He had once entered it with the police, looking for a missing member of Helena's upper stratum. What he would always remember about it was the utter silence, the addicts lying in single bunks in a sleep motionless and deep as death, the air thick and sweetish. The missing member of Helena's upper stratum was, of course, no longer there. Ah Sam, when questioned, was Orientally blank.

"I always liked the Chinese here," my father said. "They knew when to keep quiet. It's a virtue in anybody."

The fine thing about this town, he went on, was that it was more than just a place in which to exist. It was one in which every day was a new adventure. Because he himself was then young, with all the world, as he thought, before him? That might have had something to do with it, he admitted.

"But where else," he said, "could you start a day by chatting for half an hour with United States Marshal X. Beidler on that corner over there and hearing him talk about that night in Virginia City in 'sixty-three when Colonel Wilbur F. Sanders made the speech calling for the execution of George Ives, and then have lunch with Colonel Sanders himself at the Montana Club, and spend the afternoon interviewing Jim Hill about the building of his Great Northern Railroad and writing a story about it, and wind up at Ming's Opera House seeing Edwin Booth and Lawrence Barrett in *Othello*?"

I didn't know then what a rhetorical question was, but this surely was a long one.

Presently we were passing the elegantly comfortable mansion at Eighth Avenue and Ewing Street that Colonel Sanders, a justly prosperous lawyer and a United States Senator, had built to house his large family.

"He could have been much richer than he was," my father said, "but he preferred to be honest and happy. A man like Clark, who said he never bought anybody who wasn't for sale, could never understand him, but he understood Clark. He warned Montana people a dozen times what would happen if they started taking Clark's kind of corruption for granted, and he was right. He stood at a sort of crossroads. When Montana followed Clark instead of Sanders, it made a mistake it may never get over. Some time we'll come over here to a session of the Legislature, and you'll see how it works. The lobbyists pass more laws than the legislators. It all goes back to that Clark-Daly Senate fight when a man who wouldn't take a bribe was thought of as a sucker, a fool."

His indignation subsided.

"I covered X. Beidler's funeral at Ming's Opera House. The Colonel was the orator of the day, of course, and nobody cared that his voice wasn't as clear as usual. Nobody so much as whispered, either, during the hour he talked. I always thought I was a fairly tough reporter, but I was shedding a tear myself along with all the others when he came to the finish—'Brave Pioneer! To true occasions true!' That was Sanders, too. Do you really think you realize how much guts it took for Sanders to stand there that night in Alder Gulch and tell the miners they should hang George Ives? Any one of twenty of Plummer's men might have shot him. It took just as much guts, in a different way, for him to hold out for decency in politics. Not that it did anything for him," my father added, sounding bitter again, "except to leave him with a clean conscience."

He was silent for a while as we turned back toward the Gulch, and then he said what must have been in his mind as we walked.

"You have to be careful about time. It's tricky. I suppose there were days when nothing much was going on here, but somehow they've all faded out. Those sleighs going from one party to another on New Year's afternoon, eggnog and oyster suppers. I can still hear the sleigh bells. On summer nights like this one you could see the carriages moving up the Gulch and the pony phaetons whipping across the valley. People had manners and dignity, and not just the Southerners. Even the girls in the Castle had manners."

"The Castle?"

"That building over there," my father said, pointing to a brick ruin near the head of the Gulch. It did indeed have the shape of a castle. "It was what used to be known as a house of ill repute. I don't think they ever closed the doors there. If you wanted to, you could just sit around and listen to the piano and talk with one old friend or another, maybe a business friend from Anaconda. The gamblers had manners, too. The honest ones, I mean. The others didn't last long. Some of the old-school faro dealers still wore broadcloth and diamond studs—they could always pawn the diamonds when the luck turned bad. Nowadays even an honest gambler gets thrown into jail if they catch him, but I'd have trusted one of the old, honest ones ahead of any politician I can think of."

A fine place indeed, my father repeated, that city of Helena that was the love of his youth and for which he named his daughter.

"There it was," he went on, "the richest town per capita in the United States, just before the Panic of 'ninety-three, thanks to all that Last Chance Gulch gold, and the smart old merchants, but it had room for a kid reporter like me from New York State who made only enough to live on, and frontiersmen who hadn't had their hair cut since they started walking west from Missouri."

All of a sudden we were in front of the *Independent* office again.

My Father's Town

"Well, let's go in," my father said finally.

We did, and he exchanged greetings with old-timers on the staff. It was a grimy hole that did not compare, I thought, with the *Missoulian*'s city room. But it acquired a kind of magic when my father said, "My desk was over in that corner." Just as I was imagining him arriving there on a November day in 1889, he was taking a large bound volume from a shelf. It was a file of the *Independent* for November, 1889, and as I looked over his shoulder I saw that he was examining it to see what was reported in its columns the day after the young reporter from New York State arrived just in time to be, technically, a pioneer. The lead story, of course, was that Montana Territory had become the State of Montana. A telegram from James G. Blaine, Secretary of State, in Washington, to Governor Joseph K. Toole, of Montana, said so. Former President Grover Cleveland had called on President Benjamin Harrison, whose son lived in Helena. The Democratic *Independent* was gloating over a defeat suffered by Republicans in Ohio. . . .

"Well," said my father as we walked back to the hotel, "that's that."

It was nine o'clock, but the light still shone on the Big Belt Mountains to the east while the Valley of the Prickly Pear filled with shadow and a horse drawing a carriage clop-clopped down the Gulch past the building that had been Tommy Cruse's bank.

"We used to call it the Queen City of the Rockies," my father said, with the gruffness of one trying to be casual, "and we were right."

131

XIV

Exit Old West, Not Laughing

NONE OF US SAID IT, but we were all sure of it. For a few minutes, this January morning in 1922, the Old West would be coming back. The man had killed somebody, and so he too was to die. In half an hour they were going to hang him on the bright new yellow gallows in the county jail yard. Even now the early morning mist was rising off the river. We walked faster. Any young student of Montana's history who missed this would never forgive himself.

The Old West did return to us now and then, of course—at county fairs with Indians and stagecoaches and cowboys in mock combat—but something clearly was missing on those occasions. They were like movies which, however realistic, were not real, whereas Montana as a Territory and a State had been baptized in blood. Murder had been forthright, justice summary; Boone Helm, savage killer, versus X. Beidler, Vigilante. Closer to our own time, but still too early for us, Missoula in the '90's had seen a "hanging match" of proportions all but legendary—that quadruple execution of four murderous Indians by a sheriff (very old, now, and no longer sheriff) who dispatched them with great skill from a single drop in this very jail yard. Veterans dwelt long and lovingly on everything about it, remembering how the town had throbbed with carnival spirit for days before, how people

132

filled the saloons and gambling houses and paraded through the red light district right up to the climactic hour.

There had been glamor then—the Old West. And now, very soon, we'd be seeing for ourselves. For a fleeting moment, charged with grim romance, we would know a phase of which we had been cheated by one short generation.

Of course, certain allowances had to be made. This Joe Vuckovich who was about to die had not killed a man while holding up a stagecoach. He had shot a woman who wouldn't have him. He had not, with guns blazing, defied the bloodhounds of the law. He had been caught when, exhausted and hungry, he crept out of the brush and begged for food at a ranch house.

But, for our generation, the case would serve. Having killed, he was a killer. Moreover, he had "slain in animal passion"—the judge who sentenced him said so. Above all, he was a foreigner, and a Latin at that, and therefore inscrutable and dangerous. "A fiend incarnate," the county attorney had called him in his summation to the jury. So Joe Vuckovich would do.

Now the snow was falling lightly, muffling the sound of our hurrying steps. No roisterers roamed the streets, but we couldn't expect too much. The gambling houses and open saloons were long since gone, the red light district at least boarded up. Probably, we guessed, this execution would lack the festive spirit, the glad triumph of law and order, of the old open street hangings. Time had cheated us in that, and it was too bad. Still, there was a certain mystery in this silence as of a place apart where the living would briefly meet the dead. It might even be better this way. We would soon see.

In the dawn's half-light the stockade was dim, enormous, and at its entrance a man was taking engraved cards from other men who stood in a shuffling line. The law specified only a few witnesses at executions, but that was obviously nonsense. Hadn't eight thousand people seen Boone Helm hanged in Virginia City? Besides, our sheriff was running for re-election. The formal invitations had gone out by the score.

But they had gone only to voters. "Get the hell out of here," the deputy taking the cards said to us. But then he looked at a tree near the stockade and winked. A branch of the tree hung over the wall of yellow pine boards. Then we were standing inside, and it was very quiet.

Very odd, that silence. In the murky, strange light we saw a hundred people we knew, but somehow they looked different now, and they did not speak to us nor we to them. Instead we stared at a platform and two upright posts supporting a cross-beam and, dangling from the center of the cross-beam, a yellow noose. The rope disappeared into a hole in the beam and came out at one end of it, from which it ran down to an anvil perched on a little supporting ledge. Under the ledge was a stick that, pulled out by a string, would drop the anvil, jerking the body into the air. At one side was a little house like a privy; in it would be several persons, of whom one—the sheriff or a deputy—would pull the string, so that no one but themselves would know who had actually done the hanging.

It was a fancy arrangement, all right. A little disturbing, too. Had there been anything like that in Alder Gulch? We knew there had not been. And why should a hangman hide in a little house like a privy? On the old frontier, hanging had been a proud art.

Someone did speak, finally. It was the old man who, as sheriff in the '90's, had hanged the four Indians.

"It ain't goin' to work," he pronounced in a rasping, contemptuous voice. "Why don't they just kick the box out from under him?"

Why not, indeed? That was how the books and surviving witnesses said men were hanged in the old days.

No one answered. The current sheriff, fussing importantly with the anvil, like a ham actor who can't do a simple thing simply, looked around and frowned. He had spent a lot of time preparing this show. Yet his face was very pale and, even in this cold air, he was sweating. Tradition and the books said that a sheriff should be cool and efficient, like little X. Beidler, a craftsman. Someone coughed, nervously. The courthouse bell struck seven times. The sheriff walked over to the jail and went in, and the hundred of us in the shadow seemed to strain after him, waiting. Matches flared; cigarettes glowed. The eastern sky was lightening, silhouetting men with guns along the rim of the stockade.

That was more like it. Just so had armed men stood by to prevent a rescue when Boone Helm swung in Alder Gulch.

But the old sheriff was jeering again. "Who d'they think's goin' to try and save him? The marines? A special deputy gets paid, though, eh? And he's got a vote, eh?"

Someone laughed hoarsely at that, then stopped laughing, suddenly, and a long murmur came out of the open-mouthed faces in the shadow. The jail door had opened. Figures appeared in the doorway, gathered in a group that moved in a black blur down a snow-cleared path toward the platform. The sheriff, a robed minister, two deputies and, between the deputies, a man in a cheap black suit—a very little, black-haired man, with a swarthy face. For a second the straining eyes seemed to go past him, looking for someone else.

But no, it was the little man they were going to hang, because there were straps around his body above the elbow and at the wrist, and his legs were hobbled with a loose strap around the calves. The killer. They stopped beside the platform, and the little man looked at a pine box on the ground, and for a second his face was not so swarthy. Then he looked up at the noose. It was swaying a little in the dawn wind. The deputies boosted him up onto the platform where the sheriff stood beside the noose.

The sheriff cleared his throat with an echoing cough, trying to sound casual.

"Anythin' to say, Joe?"

The little man husked his throat, too, but the voice that came out of it was a kind of squeak. He hoped the man who got him into this, Christ would burn him in the fire. The sheriff looked at the minister. The minister looked at the sky and intoned a petition to the Father of mercies and the God of all comfort. Was the little man listening? He walked under the noose, inclined his head toward it, and the sheriff tightened it around his neck, the knot under the ear.

"*Back* of the ear," the old sheriff muttered. "Put that knot back of the ear, you stupid bastard, so's it won't slip."

The sheriff left the knot where it was. A deputy handed him a black mask and he covered the little man's face with it, tying the strings at the back of the head.

Now the murmur swelled into a rustling and a jostling, because this was almost the end. In a way, it *was* the end, because, when the mask went over the little man's face, he somehow ceased to exist. He was no longer a killer. He was a small animal in an elaborate trap. The shadows nearest him stood up. The shadows behind him yelled, "Down in front!" But the voices did not sound real. Alder Gulch and the old stories were real, but this was not.

The sheriff disappeared into the little house from which the slack string ran to the stick supporting the anvil. The figure was on its toes now. The string tightened between the little house and the anvil. Nothing happened. The figure stood flat-footed again. The string tightened once more, the anvil slipped downward slightly but did not fall off its perch. It moved only enough to jerk the body up an inch or two, pulling the knot over the ear and knocking the mask askew, baring a corner of the mouth. The neck reddened with a quick surge of blood.

The old sheriff jeered again, loudly. "My God! That's good! He's sheriff an' he can't hang a man wouldn't weigh a hunnerd pounds soakin' wet!"

The sheriff came running out of the little house, his face

working with panic. He lunged at the stick with his foot, the anvil thudded to the ground, the body suspended just above the platform shot up, turned quickly from side to side, then slowly. It writhed. Foam showed at the bared corner of the mouth. The body twitched, but for how long we did not know until a doctor, watch in hand, stepped forward to the platform, gazed intently at the body, and shook his head.

"Ten minutes," the doctor said.

The body jerked again, but at longer intervals, while the blood-red receded slowly from the neck. Finally it stopped twitching altogether and was still. It was still and very small —much smaller, say, than Boone Helm must have looked at the end of a rope in Alder Gulch in 1864.

Over the stockade's rim came the winter sun, slanting across the trampled yard and filling it with cold light. "Everybody out!" a deputy bellowed, though the place already seemed empty and desolate. We wanted to hurry out of there, but we could not, because the shadows had become a mass of people trudging sideways toward the gate, still staring at the black shape between the posts. Beside the platform stood the sheriff, and now his dumb, ham-actor look was also defiant, as if he expected his audience to challenge the botch he had made.

But we didn't wait to see if anyone did. We were in a hurry because, while none of us said it, we all knew it: the Old West of Alder Gulch and Bannack, of Boone Helm and X. Beidler, had not come back, and it never would, and we might as well stop thinking about it.

Mr. McGraw's Lieutenant

A NUMBER OF PEOPLE in my town had nicknames by which they were better known than by those given to them at birth. For reasons less than weighty in the long view of history, but important to me because he might just be looking on from another world and be inclined to chide me for what I am about to say, I will write of this one as Postcard Smith, so called because he ran a stationery store opposite the ball park. He was a little man who had dreamed of being a big-league ballplayer, but who never made it. Among the reasons for this was his height: five feet two inches.

So, instead, he umpired the local town-team games, coached and watched the kids, was (with the exception of the *Missoulian*'s Ray T. Rocene) Missoula's leading authority on baseball lore, and knew the old Spalding and Reach baseball *Guides* by heart. Furthermore, he was the self-appointed scout in our territory for John McGraw's New York Giants, to whom he was said to send reports on the minor-league and semipro players he saw in his wanderings around the Northwest.

In the tiny office in his store were envelopes that were not part of his stock in the trade. They bore the Giants' address—Polo Grounds, New York City, N.Y.—in one corner. Looking back now, I can guess that these envelopes enclosed routine acknowledgments of Postcard's doubtless gratuitous tips. Maybe they were letters signed by John McGraw himself!

From the second-story window of the *Missoulian-Sentinel* office in those pre-radio days, a leather-lunged citizen used to proclaim World Series play-by-play details through a megaphone after getting flashes from The Associated Press wire over which George M. Reeves presided. But for expert analysis in the street, the local fans listened to Postcard.

"Art Nehf'll come in with his curve this time," Postcard would say when the count stood at 3 and 2. He was, of course, speaking of the Giants' great left-handed pitcher.

"Nehf comes in with his curve for strike three!" the announcer would bellow through his megaphone a moment later, and we would gaze at Postcard with awe. Yes, if he hadn't been so tiny, he would have been a major-league star and later a great genius-manager, like Connie Mack or John McGraw. We were sure of it.

One spring in the early 1920's, a Missoula boy displayed unmistakable signs of more than ordinary talent as a second baseman. Postcard spent hours with him, drilling grounders at him, showing him how to pivot on the double play, and then sent him over to Butte to play in a semipro league. Just as Postcard predicted, this youngster, Eddie Bennett, began to break up games there, and soon the Butte papers were full of stories about his dazzling play.

When he had assembled a fistful of these stories, Postcard sent them off to the home office of the Giants. And apparently the Giants had been following Eddie, because one day Postcard got a letter saying the Giants would give Eddie a once-over at their Texas training camp.

On a late winter morning Eddie took off for Texas and, as Postcard assured us, certain success. At the station Postcard made a speech, gave the boy some last-minute advice and a new pair of spiked shoes. He then took out subscriptions to the New York papers in whose sports pages he would read of Eddie's inevitable progress to stardom.

When two weeks passed, he placed a bulletin board in the window of his shop, and on the board he tacked all clippings from the training camp that mentioned Eddie. "Bennett singled to left off Art Nehf yesterday in a game between the regulars and the rookies." "Bennett went far to his right to rob Frank Frisch of an almost certain single over second base." But then the bulletins became fewer, and Postcard seemed worried.

"The boy must be injured," he said.

Then there were no clippings at all, and there came a day when Postcard's door was locked. A sign written in a shaky hand said: "Closed until further notice." Someone came up with the answer, a note in the bible of baseball's periodicals, the *Sporting News:*

"Eddie Bennett is a flashy kid who looked good until the pitchers, and John McGraw, made the old and unpleasant discovery. You can be the greatest fielding second baseman who ever lived, but if you can't hit a curve ball. . . ."

Eddie must already have written the news to Postcard, who would not or could not face us. However, he did finally come back to his store. Some of the rougher kidders among the town sports had quite a time jeering at him. "When's Eddie Collins coming home?" they would ask. And, "Do we get a look at your Rogers Hornsby soon?"

He turned on his tormenters at last. "Next Saturday," he said, "and I'll be there to meet him."

So, on Saturday, we were all at the station. Eddie climbed off the train, with his cardboard suitcase and a Texas training camp tan, but looking somehow pale beneath that tan, and more than a few months older.

The boy saw the crowd and was startled. Then he looked at Postcard, who seemed suddenly aged and beaten, a fallen sage. Eddie threw his arms around the little man and said, "I'm sorry I didn't make good for you, Postcard, but it's good to be home."

Some of the sports began to look ashamed. How could they help it as they watched the still teen-age kid whose chief concern clearly was an old man now openly weeping? We were all embarrassed, and we looked to Eddie to save the situation.

With the little man's place in the community hanging in the balance, Eddie said, "You know what Mr. McGraw said to me just before I left? He said, 'Give my regards to Postcard Smith. Tell him I want him to keep on scouting ballplayers for me.' "

Postcard brightened perceptibly.

Eddie went on with it. "Mr. McGraw said, 'It wasn't Postcard's fault he didn't realize you couldn't hit a curve. Up in that thin air in the mountains, a ball don't curve much. You don't learn to hit it.' "

Postcard was almost alive again.

Eddie put on the finishing touch. "The last thing Mr. McGraw said to me was, 'I doubt there's a smarter judge of baseball between the Twin Cities and the Coast than Postcard Smith. Tell him that for me."

Did Postcard believe that large, handsome white lie? I didn't know then, nor do I know now. What I do remember is that when the parade started down Higgins Avenue toward the little stationery store, Postcard's recent detractors were standing in renewed awe of him and setting up a cheer for the kid who had gone to the far places, got one hit off the great Art Nehf, robbed Frank Frisch of a hit, and was not afraid to come home.

City Room

THE OFFICE OF THE *Missoulian*, as I have said, was as much my home as any other, for me an unceasingly fascinating place from the day I first entered it. Into it came the great outside world, on The Associated Press wire chattering in an alcove where George M. Reeves, lightning-fast telegrapher, transformed dots and dashes into typed bulletins. Piled on a table in the corner were the newspapers from the big cities—the "exchanges"—telling of life as lived elsewhere by foreign correspondents, columnists, drama critics, sports writers, their names by-words as well as by-lines. Who knows where one's education begins? But I believe that mine began here.

"Read those papers and see what you can learn," said French T. Ferguson, the *Missoulian*'s managing editor. "But don't start trying to imitate anybody in particular, or you'll get mixed up."

Mr. Ferguson, who as a young man had emigrated to Montana from Illinois, was slight and of medium height. He endlessly rolled straw-colored cigarettes, wore gold-rimmed eyeglasses and a green eyeshade, wrote editorials for the *Sentinel*, conducted a lively column entitled "The Oracle" for the *Missoulian* (a sort of local counterpart of Franklin P. Adams' "Conning Tower" in the New York *World*), supervised the news gathering and make-up for both papers, worked from 8 A.M. until well into the evening, and described himself as

142

lazy. If my father was my major mentor, he was also a figure of some awe, at least in the office. Mr. Ferguson, sometimes severe, frequently aphoristic, was instructive on a different level.

I stood before his desk on the first morning of a high school vacation during which my aptitude, if any, for the newspaper life was to be tested. Mr. Ferguson counted out twelve pennies and handed them to me. "You will weigh yourself on twelve different weighing machines around town, note the discrepancies in the machines, and see what kind of story it makes," he said, and cautioned me to eat and drink nothing while on this assignment.

The story it made was a somewhat heavily jocular one, which to my great satisfaction was printed almost as written.

"Do you think the story proved anything?" Mr. Ferguson asked me at the end of the day.

I said I supposed it proved that people should be careful about taking things for granted.

"That was the idea," said Mr. Ferguson. "It applies especially to would-be newspaper reporters."

I was not yet equipped to handle anything remotely important in the way of straight news, and I might have grown restless if Mr. Ferguson's supply of feature story ideas had not been inexhaustible. When they were unsuccessfully executed, it was my fault usually, although not always.

"A Mrs. Deschamps, down in Grass Valley, has just given birth to her twentieth child," he said one morning. "You might go and see her about it."

I did, and finally got around to asking her the obvious question.

"Difficult?" said Mrs. Deschamps, who was constructed along the lines of a French-Canadian earth mother. It was no more difficult, she said, but more tersely, than having a bowel movement. I reported back to Mr. Ferguson.

He sighed.

"It is one of the misfortunes of our profession," he said, "that a good deal that is interesting cannot be reported in newspapers exactly as it is said and done. You may live to see the day when it is, but in the meantime you may as well cultivate the art of euphemism. Perhaps you can have Mrs. Deschamps say that giving birth to her twentieth child was no more arduous than drinking a glass of that terrible dandelion wine they make down there."

He was not always so calm. A few moments after I turned in what I regarded as a witty account of a weird cult's revival meeting, he summoned me. A blue pencil line ran through the story. His gaze was cold.

"I should not have thought it necessary to tell you," he said, "that a reporter does not make fun of *any body's* religion, no matter how funny it seems to him. Who are you to pass judgments?" He relented somewhat. "That also goes for certain things that people get foolishly sentimental about, like the schools they went to, and dogs, and the virtue of womanhood, or anyhow American womanhood of a certain class."

That summer and the next, while I was still occupied with little feature stories, I could observe my highly professional elders. It was as important a part of my education as any. It would be years before I fully realized how lucky I was—that in this little city room were men who would have served well on any newspaper in the country.

Presiding over the telegraph desk was the low-voiced, efficient Ralph Swartz, who expertly read the copy and wrote the heads for about half of the *Sentinel*. The *Sentinel*'s city editor, Eddie Rosendorf, ran the city desk with dispatch and a certain waggish touch that brightened a paper on a day when there happened not to be much news. Reporter Jim Faulds covered hotels, conventions and other local matters with a deceptively easygoing countryman's air that commanded the confidence of people who regarded him on first meeting as an old friend and thereafter submitted their news to him without being asked. Mrs. Bessie K. Monroe, the *Missoulian-Sentinel*'s Bitter Root Valley correspondent in Hamilton, sixty miles away, phoned and wrote in stories, tips and features with a tireless, round-the-clock accuracy. "The Montana Nellie Bly," my father used to call her, with affectionate admiration. And there was Ray T. Rocene.

He was the wonder of our paper, this lean, intense, fast-working man who drummed at his typewriter like a frenzied pianist and on any given day wrote half a dozen stories besides assembling the sports section and turning out his "Sports Jabs," a column read throughout the Northwest. Forestry service and railroad news comprised most of his reportorial circuit outside sports. He covered it—train wrecks, forest fires, conservation projects—with unfailing skill and speed. But sports were his passion as a newspaperman, and had been so since he, a child of Swedish immigrant parents, joined the *Missoulian* staff in 1916. He remains one of the half-dozen finest sports writers I have ever read, his integrity shining through every line, his authority and style enlivening the literally countless baseball, football and boxing pieces which kept local sports fans better informed than newspaper readers in many a place much larger. He frequently angered University of Montana athletic coaches with his candid appraisals of their performance. Inevitably they came to value his advice. He described a "fixed" fight exactly as he saw it and was threatened with extinction by the manager of one of the participants.

"Go over to the hardware store across the street, get a gun, and shoot him in the belly," said the *Missoulian*'s editor, Martin Hutchens, reaching for a voucher on the *Missoulian*'s till. Ray didn't need anything like that, then or ever. Meeting the murderous manager on the street, he stared him into speechlessness.

We were a happy office and, I think, a good one. (Even

the neophyte feature writer, on vacation from high school, early included himself in that "we.") To be sure, the *Missoulian-Sentinel* was a "Company paper," which is to say, the Anaconda Copper Mining Company then held a controlling interest in it, as it did in most Montana dailies. But the *Missoulian*, at least in my father's time, enjoyed a high degree of autonomy. It frequently opposed political candidates supported by other Company papers. When, in 1919, the Chancellor of the University of Montana suspended an economics professor about to publish a book criticizing The Company's virtually tax-free status, the *Missoulian* defended the professor. I recall no story suppressed or distorted on orders from The Company, although former United States Senator Burton K. Wheeler—whom the *Missoulian* despised, and vice versa—might have had a different view of this.

"I don't have to read the *Missoulian!* I can smell it!" the Senator used to bellow when out on the hustings.

"Some day Mr. Wheeler will come to a crossroads in his career, and when he arrives there you will see him taking the opportunist's path," my father would say when I offered a word in praise of the then liberal Mr. Wheeler, a courageous United States District Attorney in Butte, a progressive Senator in the 1920's.

Mr. Wheeler, when his political career abruptly ended in 1946, was contentedly accepting the support of The Company.

Editor Martin Hutchens was one of the last of the old-school "personal" western editors, and on occasion he could be very personal indeed. Directly across West Main Street, in a second-story office facing his own, was the local headquarters of the Industrial Workers of the World. They, including their officers, were regularly denounced on the *Missoulian*'s editorial page as murderers and thieves—as, indeed, they were, despite a romanticizing tendency now to portray the I.W.W. as a Robin-Hood-like band. The local I.W.W. sent word to Editor Hutchens that it would be an easy gun shot from their office to his. The Editor put a Smith & Wesson revolver in his desk drawer and left his window shade up. The I.W.W. sent word again, this time to the effect that they respected his courage. The armed truce remained unbroken.

The Editor could be rough on his own staff, too, when he thought it advisable. That the *Missoulian-Sentinel* had no local daily paper competition was no excuse, he held, for slipshod practice. When an eight-column, Page 1 headline in the *Missoulian* appeared later in the day, by accident, in the first press run of the *Sentinel*, the building shook with his wrath; even Miss Margaret Marshall, the Editor's secretary, as calmly efficient as she was beautiful, appeared for once to be alarmed. Advertisers who ventured to suggest news treatment or ask favors never did so again. In moments of crisis—for instance, a politician charging victimization at the hands of a reporter—the Editor stood behind his man against the outsider, however he might later deal with the reporter. Not for nothing had the Editor been trained in the Pulitzer tradition.

So we all worked hard, and the days and nights went joyfully. In due time I was allowed to work later shifts, much to my pleasure. There was something special about the office then, the green-shaded lamps concentrating the light on the paper-strewn desks, the cigarette smoke curling away into the shadows. Now and then I tried rolling a cigarette myself, in the manner of Mr. Ferguson, if I had reason to think my father was not coming into the city room. When he did, in that relaxed time after the paper had gone to bed, it might be to tell a story about traveling with William Jennings Bryan in the presidential campaign of 1896. Or George Reeves would spin a tale of his days with The Associated Press in South Carolina. Or Ray Rocene would dip back into the years and his astounding memory to reconstruct a prize fight, round by round.

In that city room, night lent an extra glamor, an excitement, to encounters that would have been more nearly routine in daytime. Late in an evening when I happened to be alone in the office, a tall, well-built, well-dressed man came in and asked to see the *Missoulian* for October 5, 1892. I found it for him, and he said, "See this?" as he pointed to a paragraph announcing that Emmett Dalton, youngest of the Dalton brothers who had memorably set out to raid a bank at Coffeyville, Kansas, was about to die.

"He didn't, though," the man said. "That's me."

The city room was suddenly a street in that Kansas town where nine people, including Emmett's brothers, Bob and Grattan, died in a roar of gunfire and Emmett himself, wounded, was saved from lynching only by a quick-thinking coroner who told the townsfolk that Emmett, too, had died. Facing the sometime bandit, I trembled a bit but tried not to show it. This, it occurred to me, was like meeting one of Henry Plummer's gang in person. Wouldn't a genuine Dalton as soon shoot you as look at you?

However, Mr. Ferguson's admonitions about credulity came to the fore.

"How do I know you're Emmett Dalton?" I asked. "He went to the penitentiary for a long time."

"Fourteen years," the man said, and produced evidence: letters, clippings, pictures. I wished that someone would come back to the office, Ray Rocene or Mr. Ferguson, but no one did, and so I went to the morgue, or library, and looked into the Dalton file. Some fairly recent pictures of Emmett Dalton were certainly pictures of this man. And then he offered the final proof. He was in Missoula to lecture in advance of a crime-doesn't-pay movie, "Beyond the Law," in which he had the leading role.

Hearing this, I sensed a distinct let-down. None of Harry Plummer's boys would have gone straight as Emmett Dalton had done. I kept asking questions, as Mr. Ferguson had told me a reporter should do, and at last he came up with an answer suggesting that neither he nor the world had suddenly become perfect. Was he really sorry about all of his past? Would he relive any part of it if he could?

"Only if I had to," said Emmett Dalton. "If anybody depending on me needed food or clothes, I'd sure as hell steal it, I certainly would."

I felt a lot better as I sat down to write a story about him.

Sometimes I would walk home through the summer night with my father, because I liked to hear him tell stories of the old days, although there was a period during the I.W.W. troubles when he would not allow me to be with him. He walked alone, carrying his Smith & Wesson in his pocket. Sometimes I stopped in at the all-night grill on West Main Street, a busy lunch-and-supper spot for people who worked dull, ordinary, daytime hours in stores and such places. But at midnight the grill had a different atmosphere altogether. Then we who had helped to write two newspapers during the day and the evening, and in a sense had been around the world, met to talk over that world's events. Others, no more slaves than we to workaday respectability, drifted in and out: the old-time sheriff, Bill Houston, who had conducted the hanging of those four Indians back in 1890; the Bitter Root Kid, still trying to explain his knockout at the hands of Ever Hammer, the Chicago lightweight, but not exactly ashamed of it, because Ever Hammer in turn had been knocked out by the great Benny Leonard; a girl or two from West Front Street, her night's work done. My mother, at home, would be fretting about these late hours—"When does the boy sleep, Martin?"—but my father would not be fretting.

"You never really know a town until you know it after midnight," he used to say. And, "The more kinds of people you meet, the more you get out of life. Mind you, you don't have to like everybody, and you'd be a fool if you did, but it's well to try to understand them."

A number of kinds of people came into the *Missoulian* office—some of whom could be turned over to even a fledgling reporter. One morning every summer there arrived the Human Fly, a small, tough man with enormously muscled forearms and gnarled fingers. With him was a large, silent, unhappy-looking woman. The Fly's opening speech varied by scarcely a word from year to year. He was the world's champion in his field. Who else had climbed up the side of the Woolworth Building in *New York City*, story by story, without a net? At seven o'clock this evening he would once more favor Missoula by ascending its First National Bank Building. The *Sentinel* would do well to advise its readers of the opportunity to see the champion Fly at work, at no greater cost to them than what they chose to put into a basket passed by Mrs. Fly.

The Fly's exit line, as he stood up to leave the city room, never changed.

"You know why I'm not climbing the library here?"

The reporter knew, but pretended not to.

"Too many stories in it," said the Fly. "Get it? S-t-o-r-i-e-s, like in books."

"That's a good one, Fly," the reporter always said.

At 7 P.M., on the minute, the Fly would be standing on the sidewalk outside the First National Bank Building, clad in sports shirt, white linen trousers and tennis shoes. He would wait there while the suspense and the audience grew, then move with utmost agility up the first three stories; pause, seemingly baffled; appear to lose his footing, while the crowd gasped; go on quickly to the top cornice, and into an open window, returning in a few moments through the interior of the building to take a bow on the front steps and watch Mrs. Fly pass the basket while public appreciation of his great feat was still fresh.

One summer evening, instead of observing the Fly all the way to the top of the building, I watched Mrs. Fly. Did a slight flicker of hope cross her face when the Fly pretended to slip? It would make a neat short story, I thought. Unhappy Mrs. Fly. A shoelace surreptitiously loosened in a tennis shoe. . . . And what, I thought next, if the Fly *did* fall, right now? It wouldn't be a short story for a magazine. It would be a news story, a big one, for the next day's *Missoulian*, a genuine thriller. I knew a moment of guilty excitement bordering on anticipation. I spoke of this the next morning to Mr. Ferguson.

"It is distressing when tragedy occurs," he said, looking impassively out of the window and rolling a cigarette. "All we can do then is to report it as accurately and as interestingly as possible. And, of course, if we should be so fortunate as to have someone right on the scene at the time. . . ."

It also fell to me to write annually a small story that appeared—or, rather, wrote itself—every Decoration Day. The story said that someone, on that day, would go to the Missoula Cemetery to place flowers on the grave of an actress who had died in Missoula, suddenly and without friends, shortly after the turn of the century. The actress had been a member of a troupe headed by Nat Goodwin, the frequently married Broadway comedian who not only had gone heartlessly on and left her to perish on the frontier but had made a light-hearted remark when her fate was reported to him. The story would also recall that Goodwin never dared to appear again on a stage in Missoula lest western defenders of betrayed feminine innocence take vengeance upon him.

"I gather from reading your story," said Mr. Ferguson, "that you are not entirely sure of what actually happened."

I admitted this.

"It may be just as well," said Mr. Ferguson, "since the press does not as yet publicize details relating to abortion."

Mr. Ferguson must, I thought, occasionally grow weary of planning minor assignments for his vacation-time neophyte reporter. I was mistaken.

"It seems to be a fact of human nature, whether a praise-worthy one or not I do not pretend to say," he began one morning, "that most people like to see their names in a news-paper—assuming that they have not suddenly found them-selves in the role of defendants in embarrassing circumstances in a courtroom."

He then drew up for me a list of lawyers and doctors on whom I was to call at more or less regular intervals. Almost without exception, I noted, they were among the least emi-nent and least successful practitioners in their fields.

"That is the point," said Mr. Ferguson. "They are lone-some. Some of them were important in their day. They have a lot to remember. They also have time to get around. With-out making a nuisance of yourself, you can see them often enough to catch them when they feel like talking, which will generally be the case, especially among the lawyers. A lawyer who does not like to talk has no business being a lawyer in the first place."

If my small-time lawyers and doctors were startled and us-ually suspicious at being called upon by a sixteen-year-old reporter who had nothing in particular to ask them, I in turn was puzzled by them. How did they earn a living? The two county judges now and then tossed to the lawyers the hope-less task of defending penniless defendants against whom the prima-facie evidence was overwhelming. The doctors' initial assumption that I sought a cure for an ailment then known as "a social disease" was flattering to one of my ten-der years. (This was the era when a male was not considered quite a man until he had been thus afflicted.) It also said a good deal about the general run of their practice.

But Mr. Ferguson, as usual, was right. These worn, un-successful men did get around, and they did like to talk. Such as it was, most of their news was tidbits—"Mr. and Mrs. John Smith, of Polson, are guests this week of Mr. and Mrs. John Doe of 100 Daly Avenue"—but it had its legitimate place in a newspaper most of whose readers were acquainted with one another. And once in a while a visit produced, quite surprisingly, a story that was more than an item.

In his barnlike office in the First National Bank building was the tall old doctor with the gray celluloid collar, spotted Windsor tie, cigarette-stained fingers, and moustache yellow as the parchment diplomas on the walls of his seldom-consulted consulting room. The doctor, I said by way of an opening gambit, rolled cigarettes with a deftness approaching that of my boss, Mr. Ferguson. The doctor was more than a little indignant.

"*I* learned to roll cigarettes, my boy, because for many years I lived and practiced in lands where manufactured cigarettes were not to be bought for a king's ransom," he said. I had read this phrase in romantic fiction, but I had never heard it spoken. I apologized for my unfortunate remark. He forgave me and went on to tell a story, which I did not believe, of crossing the African veldt with a train of mules to whose tails burning brands were tied—"to frighten the natives, and sinister rascals they were," the doctor explained. "Lord Kitchener was not what I would call a sociable man, but he thanked me graciously for saving several hundred of his men during the Boer War from death by sleeping sickness induced by the tsetse fly."

While I was wondering why the doctor had not received the Nobel Prize for this feat, he said casually, "Did you know that a cousin of Wild Bill Hickok lives down the Bitter Root Valley? He was with Bill in the McCanles fight"—an interesting bit of mayhem early in the Hickok career in Nebraska. I all but ran out of the office to investigate this unlikely lead. The old doctor was right, though, and there was a story. . . .

More often there was no story but something that went into the memory and stuck there. An ancient Socialist and lawyer recited by heart Robert G. Ingersoll's oration on Shakespeare and his commemorative address on the Civil War dead, the voice rising and falling in artful melancholy while I sat entranced. ("They sleep in the land they made free, under the flag they rendered stainless, under the solemn pines, the sad hemlocks, the tearful willows. . . .") "A Republican and an agnostic," the ancient Socialist said of Ingersoll, "but a good man." When a youngster, he had journeyed to Butte to watch a classic duel between two great attorneys, Ingersoll and Colonel Wilbur Fisk Sanders, the old Vigilante hero, who opposed each other for six weeks in a will case of great complexity.

"How they hated Ingersoll at first in Irish-Catholic Butte, an Easterner and an unbeliever! And how they came to love him before he was through there! How could they help it when he gave his Shakespeare lecture for nothing, to help a fund for families of miners killed in an accident, and donated a thousand dollars besides? If you live long enough, my boy, you'll find out that some of the best Christians don't always go to church or even call themselves Christians."

So it was, in that Montana town in the frontier's sunset glow, between the old and the new, with the *Missoulian* office, that smoky, ink-stained alma mater, as my home base. Life was delightful. On occasions it was magnificent, notably on election nights. Local and state elections, that is. Montana could take a presidential election or leave it alone, but within its borders politics was fiercely partisan. Montanans did not vote for X. They voted against Y. In a State whose population was preposterously small in terms of the State's size—some six hundred thousand in what was then the nation's third-largest commonwealth—all was intensely personal: politics, journalism, business, but politics above all, as anyone could see amid the hubbub in our office when the returns came in.

Opposing candidates trudged up our steep stairs to learn their fate, and sometimes were kept apart with difficulty. Congressman John M. Evans, Democrat, inevitably was there to make certain that his sure-fire platform—universal peace and no income tax—had once again successfully wooed the electorate. Mr. W. J. Babbington, the County Clerk and Recorder—he and his staff were known to the *Missoulian*'s sharp-tongued editorial page as Ali Babbington and His Forty Assistants—braved the fortress of his enemy. Joseph M. Dixon did not.

Mr. Dixon (unjustly opposed by the *Missoulian*, I later came to believe) was a distinguished man. A Republican United States Senator from 1906 to 1912, he broke with his party when he joined Theodore Roosevelt's Bull Moose mavericks and managed T.R.'s 1912 presidential campaign. A superb orator, who entered upon a discourse with a soft voice that built to a ringing, magnetic eloquence, he was also a brave politician who, alone among Montana governors, dared to challenge The Company on the tax issue—and won by appealing to the people in a popular referendum, although it meant his political suicide, The Company having its own ways of defeating him when he next ran for office.

When the election-night excitement was over on a November night in the early 1920's, my father and I were strolling along Higgins Avenue toward home. Through the doorway of the Florence Hotel came Mr. Dixon, whom an editorial in the *Missoulian* had come close to libeling the day before. I foresaw violence, in the tradition of Montana politics. But Governor Dixon, too, had been a newspaperman.

"Good evening, Martin," said the Governor.

"Good evening, Joe," said the Editor.

They shook hands and conversed amiably for a few moments about nothing. This was a lesson in practical politics as played by professionals.

There was always something to learn.

XVIII

Warriors

IF I FREQUENTLY REGRETTED that I had not known at first hand the Alder Gulch of X. Beidler, Henry Plummer, Boone Helm and other saints and sinners, it was happily apparent that there were still combative giants in my part of the earth. That they fought with fists instead of guns mattered not at all. Indeed, it was better this way, if only because they lived to fight another day, their prowess a continuing source of enjoyment to all followers of The Fancy. Even before the Legislature rescinded the ban on boxing in 1921, all sporting Montanans were aware of our State's stirring tradition of the manly art of mayhem. It had begun with the Orem-O'Neil carnage in Alder Gulch back in the early 1860's. But the tradition's liveliest home, naturally, was Butte, where Irish miners fought for the fun of it in the streets on Saturday nights. It was in Butte that Battling Nelson beat Aurelio Herrera in twenty rounds in 1904, the Mexican reviving himself with gulps of rye whiskey between rounds. It was Butte that saw miner Jack Monroe floor heavyweight champion Jim Jeffries in an exhibition bout. Above all it was Butte where a pulverizing Pole from Michigan, Stanley Ketchel, at the age of seventeen, launched the career that took him to the middleweight championship of the world.

During Montana's long boxing drought, old ringsiders warmed themselves with memories of Ketchel—how he developed his killer instinct by fighting for his life nightly in a brothel where he served as bouncer, a strenuous job in a copper camp populated largely by Irish, Finnish and Cornish miners; how, in the days of his greatness, he appeared on New York's Fifth Avenue in a fancy dressing gown and tossed peanuts to his admirers; how be knocked down the mighty Jack Johnson, fifty pounds heavier than himself; and how—it somehow seemed western and right—he was murdered in Missouri in a row about a woman.

But in Missoula we had a source of pride to match that of any Ketchel fan. We had among us the only man who ever defeated Ketchel more than once.

Maurice Thompson, rancher, did not boast about this. Maurice, soft-spoken and courteous, used to say there wasn't anything remarkable in his pair of victories over Ketchel, because Ketchel was only a beginner then—in 1903—and why shouldn't an old campaigner like himself outpoint a boy? Just the same, when he came into town from his ranch, hero-worshiping small fry followed him in the street, and when one night in 1922, nearing forty, and somewhat paunchy, he neatly won a six-round bout, we felt ourselves restored to the golden age of Corbett and Fitzsimmons.

Nor was Maurice our only hero. Still in the ring, where he had made his debut shortly after the turn of the century, was Kid Jackson, bantamweight, also getting on toward forty, a dancing master with a near-lethal punch—Kid Jackson, who never held a national title but once went ten rounds to a draw with a future lightweight champion, Ad Wolgast, and emerged from 272 bouts with no injury graver than a somewhat enlarged nose. Finally the Kid did reach forty, and in the local ball park was matched for ten rounds with a cocky, rugged young man from Spokane, approximately half the Kid's age. As he trained at the Pastime A.C., the Kid seemed lithe and swift as ever. Still, there were all those years, and that thatch of gray hair. Could he make it? We were worried.

The big night came, and in those ten rounds, without drawing a long breath, the Kid slashed his way to a victory so devastating that the young man from Spokane never was heard from again.

But in all Montana's history of organized violence within the squared circle, the afternoon of July 4, 1923, stands alone. Did it actually happen, a world's heavyweight championship fight in a tiny oil town, Shelby, on the Northern Montana prairie while a crowd of eleven thousand sat baking in a yellow pine arena built to accommodate four times that many? Who would have bet a single silver cartwheel, a year before, that Jack Dempsey would be putting his title on the line before an audience that included a former Mrs. Vanderbilt and a hundred Blackfoot Indians cheering somewhat ominously for Tommy Gibbons, a sort of hometown boy? (His home was in St. Paul, only a thousand miles to the east.)

The *Missoulian-Sentinel*, of course, proposed to cover the story in force. It was almost in our backyard, as distances go in Montana.

"This may well be a memorable adventure, gentlemen," my father said formally, as our delegation climbed into his battered Hupmobile and headed north. My father would be in general charge. Ray Rocene, then and still at this writing the *Missoulian-Sentinel*'s greatly gifted sports writer, would do the lead story. French Ferguson would find material for his "Oracle" column. I would be a sort of messenger, but maybe, with some luck, I would have a chance to write a little something around the edges of this first Big Story I had ever had anything to do with. Here, in the offing, was drama. I could not have guessed how incredible it would seem at the very time it was taking place.

A day and a half later, on July 2, we were in Shelby. The epic of the prairies was forty-eight hours away. The epic was going to occur in that yellow pine bowl over there which overshadowed the little town lying in a mile-wide valley between two low ranges of hills. That was the first and last thing about Shelby. Even if you tried, you couldn't forget the bowl that was yellow in the sun, silver in the moon, and bigger than the town.

We parked the car and turned up Main Street. Indians rode along it, back and forth, in dirty blankets and bright feathers. Cowboys stomped by, their faces burned to russet by the sun; this had been a cow town before it was an oil town. The street stank with oil spread on it to lay the dust. With rain the dust would be gray mud, but now the sun shone hotly. We moved along slowly through the crowd and its undertone of fight talk—a quizzical, sometimes angry hum. Past the Red Onion Cafe we went, past Milady's Hat & Gift Shop and the Green Light Pavilion, the King Tut Dance Hall—one-story buildings, for the most part—and beyond them shacks and tents at the town's edge; and after that, the prairie and the sky.

"Hello, Martin," a man said from the crowd. He was a friend of my father's and a member of the Shelby Chamber of Commerce; he was red-faced and a little drunk, and he wore a badge on his lapel. "Help Build Shelby," the badge asked.

My father said hello.

"Ain't going to be any fight," the man said. He seemed quite cheerful about it. "Ain't enough money left in the state for that Jack Kearns."

"He's got till tomorrow morning to raise what's coming to him and Dempsey under the contract," my father reminded him.

"The mortgages'll choke our boys before they raise it," the man said. "Besides, who's comin' to the fight if they ain't sure of seein' one?"

He was right about that. I was listening to him and also to a man sadly calling attention to Mary Ellen, the eight-horned horse. We moved along again and I stopped in front of a big cowboy and stared at him, because there weren't many cowboys in our mountainous part of the state. This one wore a five-gallon hat and a purple bandanna. The Old West, all right. On closer inspection, he turned out to be Heywood Broun, the New York *World* columnist whom I regularly read when loitering around the table covered with out-of-town newspapers in the *Missoulian* office. I did not dare to speak to him.

Then, just before we reached the hotel where we were lucky to find quarters in the basement, we passed the First State Bank of Shelby. In the doorway stood a gray-haired man smiling fixedly. That, my father said, was Mayor Jim Johnson, "Smiling Jim," who was going to lose $150,000 of his own on this fight—and all because a few oil men, sitting around one winter night five months before, had had a bright idea for publicizing their town. No phony promotion, to be sure; no selling of oil stock, though if anyone insisted on buying an oil lease. . . . No, they just wanted some publicity for Shelby, Chamber of Commerce fashion. Come out and grow up with the country. There were little models of oil rigs in the windows along the street. No one was looking at them.

It took all of ten minutes to discover what Shelby had its eye on. Shelby loved Tom Gibbons. Dempsey, in training at Great Falls, a hundred miles away, was an Easterner and an enemy. Gibbons was virtually a neighbor, a Minnesotan. He was modest and decent and a family man, the sort of fighter who takes his wife and children to his training camp because he likes to have them around.

So we stood with Shelby in the glare of his training quarters that afternoon to watch him work. You could feel people pulling for the challenger, trying to believe that he was a hitherto undisclosed giant-killer as well as a fine boxer. This wasn't easy. He had done little work in the sun, his body was pale, and he seemed more frail than he actually was. Watching him, you kept thinking of Dempsey. Once in a while during his workout Gibbons smiled at the spectators, but it was a wistful sort of smile, and never once did he look at the great yellow pine arena four hundred yards away. Suddenly I was sorry for him, the way I had been sorry for the killer at the county jail in Missoula who could see the gallows he was going to die on.

"Maybe you'd better take some notes on this," said my father. It was an electrifying hint. I moved closer to the platform where Gibbons was concluding his daily stint and his manager, Eddie Kane, was talking glibly. Tommy would not only stay off the floor but would likely knock Dempsey out, Kane said. An eastern sports writer laughed out loud when he saw me solemnly recording this prophecy. We went back to the hotel and, at a nod from my father, I sat down to write a story about our tiger killer from St. Paul. Panic shook me. How, on so little notice, was I to do justice to so momentous an occasion as this? I froze.

My father said, "You are not writing a definitive history of the Wars of the Roses. You are writing a story about a man getting ready for a fight. Take it easy."

I wrote and wrote, and about one-third of what I wrote was struck out by the heavy black pencil my father wielded. Mr. Ferguson saw me wince. "You'll be glad of it later," he said as he took our delegation's batch of copy to the Western Union wire. And I was indeed glad of it when the *Missoulian* of the next morning arrived in Shelby in late afternoon. At some point between the hotel and the Western Union, Mr. Ferguson had awarded a seventeen-year-old neophyte his first by-line. When I could stop rereading the by-line, I read the story. Thanks to that heavy black pencil my father had wielded, the story was not entirely contemptible. It was even, I admitted to myself in utmost secrecy, not the very worst story I had ever read on a sports page.

Our first day's work done, we went back to Main Street. We were always going back to Main Street. There was no other place to go. It was a comic, sad place. Around the town lurked some ladies of the evening whose best evenings were far in their past. Orchestras blared, but no one danced. For entertainment there were only the concessionaires, who lived off one another; two rodeos; and Patricia Salmon, Irish comedienne and yodeling star of the Hyland-Welty Stock Company. Patricia had big brown eyes, and also danced. The newspapermen from New York had been telling her she would be on Broadway within two years. She asked them to stop kidding her.

Drifting in the moonlight that evening, the crowd was nervous, bored, waiting for news from Great Falls, the Dempsey-Kearns headquarters. Reporters were shadowing Jack Kearns down there, asking of Dempsey's wily manager what he planned to do. Here in Shelby the owner of Mary Ellen, the eight-horned horse, was barking for dimes, but few people seemed to have a dime. Shortly after 1:00 A.M. our red-faced committeeman found us. He was a bit drunk, as he had been in the afternoon, and he still wore the badge that asked "Help Build Shelby."

"It's off for good now," he announced. "Kearns said if they'd give him at least half of the third hundred thousand the contract guarantees him, he'd gamble for the rest. But they couldn't give him half."

But the next day, the fight was on again. Kearns had taken over the books and was now the promoter. He was going to gamble for all of that last installment.

The Fourth dawned clear, with a slight breeze coming in from the baked mud flats. It was a thick, warm wind. At five o'clock, when I got up, it was very quiet in the town. I walked down the hotel corridor that was lined with cots, and out into the street where the dried oil was swirling in little brown clouds. The day before, the town had started to fill up. There was almost hope. A couple of special trains had arrived, and a number of shabby automobiles, and a small army of the curious characters who follow the big fights. God only knows how they got to Shelby, but nobody was asking questions now. The town awoke suddenly, Main Street was alive, and we stood in line for breakfast at the Red Onion Cafe.

Rumors started up and then died, in the heavy air. The fight was off again? It was not. There was lusty talk of destroying an enterprising operator from St. Paul who had imported 150 cases of near beer, removed the labels, and offered it at $1.50 a bottle. Instead, the crowd went to the Great Northern railroad station to meet Dempsey's special car, due at eleven o'clock. It came in, with curtains drawn, and went onto a sidetrack near the arena. I went back to Main Street where ticket speculators were trying desperately to unload. Fifty-five-dollar seats were looking for buyers at ten dollars. Mary Ellen's owner was still barking for dimes.

In the arena at noon, no wind stirred. Yellow acres of empty seats stretched away to a horizon of their own. The first of the preliminary fighters came on, and occupants of cheap seats stormed into the thirty-dollar section, knocking over ushers. Suddenly, outside, a roar swelled skyward. I walked to the top of the arena and looked down. Inside a barbed-wire fence were Promoter Kearns and his deputies. They were taking money through the wire from scratched hands and cramming it into satchels. Kearns, sharp-faced and sweating but still oddly dapper, was watching the satchels. Three Internal Revenue Department agents were watching Kearns. They were supposed to collect a ten percent tax. The Kearns deputies were working fast but not fast enough. The wire broke, and the mob surged through. The revenue men fired over their heads and the shots were a thin crackle in the uproar. Kearns stood closer to the satchels.

I went back to my seat as the semifinal worked to a finish, and now the heat was charged with tension. It was about 3:30. A long murmur breaking into unexpected applause was for

Dempsey as he walked down the long aisle from the top of the arena, preceded by a Chicago detective carrying an open gun in his hand. In the ring the champion laughed and talked with friends in the press rows. The West watched and hated him, the enemy from the East. A sudden shout was for Gibbons, who made a quick, nervous entrance from a trapdoor near the ring. The Indians yelled and wahooed for him—they had made him Chief Thunder Cloud a few days before and given him a fancy headdress. In the ring Dempsey peeled off his white sweater and Gibbons his robe, and they posed for the cameras. Someone tossed a pop bottle and bruised a Chicago *Tribune* photographer's ankle: Shelby's final salute to eastern journalism.

To my untutored eye it was not a good fight, and all the "moral victory" claims for Gibbons—just because he survived fifteen rounds—could not make it seem otherwise. Gibbons boxed cleverly and gamely. He could not hope to do more. Dempsey stalked and mauled him but did not bring him down. Was he really trying to? Observers disagreed then about this and have continued ever since to do so. The crowd's mood was ugly. A number of ringsiders were armed. It might well have seemed to the champion that sufficient unto the day were the retention of his title and as much of the gate as he and his manager could carry away.

In an hour it was all over, and in the dooryard of Gibbons' cottage, when he was rushed home in a wrapping of blankets, his two sons were setting off Independence Day firecrackers in patriotic unconcern. The family man had come home alive.

No line formed that night in front of the Red Onion Cafe. The shoddy cars sputtered off into the prairie, and the special trains cleared for action. The town was not yet empty, but it was desolate and tired—and dead broke. Mayor Johnson stood in a doorway, still smiling, and asked if anyone could let him have the price of a shave. It was a brave joke, and almost no joke at all. Mr. Kearns had all the money. He stood guard over it all night in the Mayor's busted bank while the revenue men weighed schemes to pry an additional tax out of him. But Mr. Kearns was too smart. He was always too smart for the local boys. In the morning Main Street heard how he had hired an engine and lit out for Great Falls while the revenue men waved attachment papers at him from the platform.

It was raining when the *Missoulian-Sentinel* delegation finished with their mopping-up stories. To kill time before we set out for home, I walked out in the rain, and, passing Gibbons' cottage, I saw him on the porch. He was throwing odds and ends into a trunk. To my surprise I found myself turning in at the gate and walking up to the porch. "Hello, there," he said agreeably. I asked him some routine questions, but he could see that I was a boy trying to be a grown-up reporter, and he answered pleasantly because he was a pleasant person.

He hadn't been hurt, he said, except when Dempsey rabbit-punched him. He talked about his family and the vaudeville tour he was going to make, but nothing was so significant to me as the way he never looked toward the arena. The Black-foot braves had come over and taken back their tribal head-dress, he said, smiling a shade sadly.

It was mid-afternoon when the *Missoulian-Sentinel* representatives and the old Hupmobile rambled out of Shelby. After the town had sunk out of sight across the prairie we could still see the arena, enormous and sodden in the rain, and beyond it a big civic auto camp where there had not been many autos. Why had it ever happened? Then one of us remembered that Shelby had hoped to sell some oil leases, and someone else laughed and said that there had been one bona fide sale. Mrs. Raymond T. Baker (formerly a Mrs. Vanderbilt) had bought a quarter section for fifty dollars, paid a two-dollar tax, reserved the oil rights to herself, and given the rest to the Negro porter on her special car.

A bank in Great Falls closed on July 9. Mayor Johnson's closed the following day, and a second Shelby bank closed in August. The State bank examiners would not say specifically that the banks had invested in the fight, but the depositors seemed to think so. Still, Shelby had one more flash, and it was far from Main Street. Florenz Ziegfeld, then producing one of his "Follies" on Broadway, had been moved to curiosity by the New York reporters' funny stories from Shelby about Patricia Salmon, the sweet yodeler of the tents. He brought her to New York with a cagey blare of Alice-in-Wonderland exploitation. Fifteen Follies girls met her at Grand Central Terminal, and Billie Burke (Mrs. Ziegfeld) took her on a lavish shopping tour. She went into the show and did not do too badly. Yodeling is a gift.

But the next—and last—time I saw her was on a June night five years later. She was trying to make a few dollars of prize money at Madison Square Garden in one of those weird dance marathons, a now fortunately defunct phenomenon of the 1920's. She had been dancing for seven days and nights, and for the last few hours her partner had been holding her up because she was then in a semicataleptic state. I almost did not place her, yet something about her was familiar. Then I recognized it: she looked like Shelby on the morning of July 5, 1923. She finally passed out altogether.

XVIII

Blood on the Bridge

"I OUGHT TO KICK BOTH OF YOU out of here for good," my father said. He was speaking to me, still a high school vacation-time reporter, and to Homer Parsons, an established if happily eccentric member of the *Missoulian*'s regular staff. Homer had arrived on the paper as a printer and gone on to become a poetry-writing news hawk who specialized in challenging the local police force, whom he despised, to fisticuffs. He seldom if ever triumphed, but his enthusiasm never dimmed.

"I ought to kick both of you out of here," my father repeated, "because everybody will think the *Missoulian* planted it. However, I don't think I will. Don't ask me why."

I was watching him carefully. It was hard to tell what he really was thinking. He was wearing his city-room face, and his voice was harsh, but somehow I sensed that Homer's and my caper, at the expense of the police and the *Missoulian*'s only local rival, did not strike him as a complete outrage.

The rival was the *New Northwest*, a weekly with a capacity for indignation about almost everything, from the weather to the sins of the Anaconda Copper Mining Company. Among its favorite targets was the *Missoulian*, to which it attributed failure to cover the news responsibly or even adequately.

Over a midnight coffee in the all-night grill on Main Street,

167

Homer and I fell to discussing our angry enemy, the *New Northwest*. Its gibes, we agreed, were becoming tiresome. If the *New Northwest* truly wanted to score a beat, said Homer, why did we not give it a genuine chance to?

I waited, while a dreamy haze came into the poet-reporter's eyes.

"It should be a beat," he suggested, "in which the *New Northwest* and my friends the police share honors equally. They deserve each other."

Within an hour the plan was sketched, in a few days it was perfected, and two weeks later, on the eve of the *New Northwest*'s publication day of Saturday, Homer and I were standing on the Van Buren Street bridge. The old Hupmobile was parked at one end of it. The night was black and silent. With a kind of affectionate care Homer opened a package, extracted a woman's torn shirtwaist, and poured over it a half pint of cow's blood acquired from a slaughterhouse on the edge of town. With a stone he anchored on the floor of the bridge a letter he had written on an office typewriter that afternoon. At the risk of seeming to lack modesty, he said, he could only describe it as a masterpiece. It read (and I quote from the newspaper in which it was to appear):

Dear Hazel:

I heard through Jim that you were in Missoula, and I want to talk it over with you. We ought to come to some kind of an agreement. But I think we had better not be seen together.

I'll wait for you tomorrow night about 1 o'clock on the Van Buren Street Bridge. Nobody goes around there then and we can talk without anybody butting in.

You know things can't go on like this forever. I can't stand that. You've get to decide between your husband and me.

O. B.

Blood on the Bridge

Descending to the bank below, we poured more blood on the rocks there, dragged a bag of stones to the water's edge, emptied it, and returned to the bridge. The dumbest member of the police force would have to recognize this as the trail of a corpse dropped from the bridge and thrown into the river. With my father's revolver, nervously taken from his desk, I fired two shot into the stream below. Homer uttered a shriek as of a woman in the throes of death. We ran to the car and in a few minutes Homer, a virtuoso of the first order, was calling his old foe the chief of police from a phone booth and, purporting to be a householder living in the vicinity of the bridge, was telling him that murder had likely been done there.

"We'll be there in five minutes," said the Chief. A portly incompetent, he was, for once, as good as his word. He and his men worked through the night assembling the evidence and reconstructing the crime. The next morning, Reporter Parsons neglected to call at the police station. The *New Northwest* man had the field to himself. When his paper reached the newsstands in the late morning, it had a clean beat: "Suspected Murder Mystifies Police." It even had, in addition to the letter Homer had left on the bridge, the text of a telegram to the Chief, sent from Helena, presumably by Hazel's husband:

DESIRE TO KNOW THE WHEREABOUTS OF MY WIFE, HAZEL STANTON. IF YOU FIND HER HOLD FOR INVESTIGATION AND WIRE AT MY EXPENSE.

WALLACE STANTON.

Homer, who had friends everywhere, had overlooked nothing except a sound excuse for having missed a murder story breaking at the most important point on his daily rounds. Mr. Ferguson and my father roared at him. If he wanted to keep his job, they told him, he had better do something extraordinary in the way of a story for our afternoon edition, the *Sentinel*. Homer hung his head, in what he deemed an appropriate gesture of shame, and promised to do his best.

Together Homer and I adjourned to the police station, where the Chief foresaw an early solution to the case. Pausing to congratulate Homer ironically on missing the biggest story of the year, he told how he and his dauntless assistants had invaded a hobo jungle not far from the Van Buren Street bridge and there had picked up a vagrant with bloodstains on his tattered clothes. They did not, obviously, pause to reflect that their hobo had merely been in a fight. With the pride of Scotland Yard bringing in a new Jack the Ripper, they fetched him to the station and booked him for homicide. Homer and I watched each other turn pale. The day wore on. Mr. Ferguson was clamoring for a story for the *Sentinel*. Homer put him off with vague hints that the *New Northwest*'s triumph was not so stunning as it appeared to be.

And then, as dusk came on, we heard it, the ominous murmur of a crowd gathering around the rickety jail from which through the years so many prisoners had escaped with ridiculous ease. Through the shadows came the words "rope" and "string him up." Homer and I asked for a private conference with the Chief. In his office we confessed. I was too insignificant for the Chief's wrath. Homer caught it in full force.

"God damn you, I've got you now!" said the Chief, with violent satisfaction. "You'll get a year for this, hoaxing the law. A year in the pen, and every cent you've got."

"Wait a minute," said the magnificent Homer. He reached into a notebook and produced a carbon of what appeared to be a signed and witnessed document. "I have here," he said, in a parody of the Chief's pomposity, "an affidavit by a couple of the boys on Railroad Avenue saying they're tired of being shaken down every Saturday night for that little poker game they run. Fifty dollars—if you're going to shake down a small-time gambler, you ought to make it bigger, Chief. Fifty-five, anyhow."

It was the Chief's turn to go a shade pale.

"All right," he said, "and get the hell out of here, and leave that paper."

"Certainly," said Homer, handing over the copy with the air of a grandee tipping a panhandler, "but remember I've got the original. Now maybe you'd better get rid of that mob out there."

The vagrant was released, and we too were at liberty if not quite at ease. There was a further confession to be made at the *Missoulian* office. It was then that my father said, "I ought to kick both of you out of here. . . ."

I was still watching him carefully a few days later as he read the *New Northwest*'s characteristically indignant follow-up story. Under the headline "It Was a Practical Joke But Maybe the Story Isn't All Told," the *New Northwest* quoted the Chief as saying that "if we can find the persons who perpetrated the hoax they will be arrested," while the county attorney blandly took credit for forestalling a lynching by sending the bloodstained shirtwaist of poor Hazel to the State University biology department for analysis. The *Missoulian* and *Sentinel* had contentedly and obliquely given the public to understand that a certain sixth sense, with which Providence endows great newspapers, had warned them to stay away from so dubious a story as this.

"You know, don't you," my father said, "that you and Mr. Parsons were taking a chance with a man's life?"

I knew it now, I said, although Homer and I had not realized it at the time.

"Don't do it again," my father said, leaving me to guess just how much he meant that word "it" to include.

The Sinister City

"Butte," Mr. Ferguson was saying, "is a place that no one should visit until he has reached a certain age."

As always when he chose not to address directly the person to whom he was speaking, he gazed out of the window while he rolled a cigarette.

"Butte," said Mr. Ferguson, "is a sinful city by conventional standards. All the recognized forms of vice are rampant, the moonshine whiskey is likely to kill anyone who is not an Irishman or a Finn, and a miner at that. The food is magnificent if you go to one of the Italian restaurants in a suburb called Meaderville. Yes, Butte is sinister. It is also fascinating. If I were considerably younger, I would join you and your friend Evan Reynolds on this expedition you are contemplating."

Mr. Ferguson was then in his forties, obviously too advanced in years for the journey that Evan and I were about to undertake. Evan and I were then eighteen.

The trip had been a long time in the planning. There was, for one thing, the matter of money. It would not do to go empty-pocketed to the city where F. Augustus Heinze had frolicked, where Marcus Daley, with a word or two at a bar about a share in a lease on his next mine, had seen to it that old friends became men of wealth.... Evan and I had hoarded fifty dollars each for a week end that would begin this very day, Friday, when we stepped on the Northern Pacific's late-afternoon train, the Butte *Stub*—a local train, as distances went in Montana. The somber old Thornton Hotel would be our Butte headquarters. The sky, or as near to it as our combined resources would take us, would be our limit.

It would be a journey the more stirring because no one, as far as I knew, ever was indifferent about Butte. It was hated, or loved, or both. It was the home of the Anaconda Copper Mining Company's raw power. The real government of Montana, as every Montanan was aware, was located on the sixth floor of the Hennessy Building, in a city that was not so much a city as a mining camp beneath whose bare, rock-soil surface ran more than two thousand miles of tunnels from which over two billion dollars in ore had been extracted in the last fifty years. As you came into it by train at night, it had—at a distance—the shiny gleam of a stage setting, its street lights and the lights at the shaft heads winking like jewels in a huge diadem. By day it was ugly as the sin about which Butte did not unduly concern itself until reform arrived in the 1940's. In the sunlight the bleak slag heaps and ore tailings on The Richest Hill on Earth reminded you that the business of this camp was the money that poured out of the ground.

What was it, I used to wonder, as others have wondered, that gave Butte its special, electrifying quality, its air of excitement suggesting that all hell might break loose at any moment? It was the altitude, said some. It was its remoteness and the effect of radio-active minerals, said others. It was the complexity of its racial pattern, said still others: the Irish, the Finns and the Cornishmen who would rather fight than eat or even drink—and the drinking in Butte had never been less than prodigious, from the miner taking his "John O'Farrell" (whiskey with beer chaser) as soon as he emerged from the depths at the end of his shift in the Never Sweat or the

Minnie Healey to the tycoons absorbing rare wines at the elegant Silver Bow Club. In the very heart of the Prohibition era, Butte was proud of its old-fashioned, swinging-door saloons. Federal marshals were regularly dispatched from Washington, D.C., to enforce Prohibition. Just as regularly, they achieved nothing, and some of them never were heard of again—they were either bribed or otherwise sent on their way—it is not impossible that bones found moldering in deep shafts of one mine or another were those of officials who had been overly zealous or insufficiently corruptible. Butte allowed that Billy Sunday, the evangelist who engaged in hand-to-hand battle with the Devil on the platform and always won three falls out of three, knew what he was talking about when he said that the bottles consumed in one week in Butte would build a stairway from Butte's highest peak down to hell's lower reaches.

Anything at all incited violence in that supercharged atmosphere. Miners fought The Company's hired gunmen— a goon squad, they would be called now—and blood ran down The Richest Hill on Earth. On an August day in 1917, Frank Little, an organizer for the Industrial Workers of the World, was dragged from the Butte boarding house where he lay with a broken leg, pulled through the streets, and hanged from a railway trestle, with the old Vigilante warning sign, 3-7-77, pinned to his corpse. Even those who despised the I.W.W. saw it as an act of consummate cruelty and cowardice and had little doubt about who had commissioned the job. Butte was seldom without the smell of death, accidental or deliberately inflicted.

At the same time, it was alive with a vibrancy all its own, and a prevailing, good-humored tolerance. On the part of The Company, this tolerance was generally recognized as having an element of calculation. The more the red light district and the gambling emporiums took of the miners' energy and money, the less were the chances of a strong labor union movement. In effect, The Company sponsored, if it did not actually license, Butte's wide-openness. Butte did not complain. Butte had room for everything and everybody. Butte was surprised by nothing.

Did a lady of Butte's upper social stratum coolly name and collect a fee of several thousand dollars for a night spent with the degenerate son of a copper king? Butte smiled. Such enterprise, on the lady's part, was in the freebooting western tradition. Obsequies were happy occasions. They began with a dutiful solemnity, grew more relaxed as a wake grew more alcoholic, and wound up with spirited horse races to and from the cemetery, after which bets were paid off and the drinking went on. When F. Augustus Heinze's personal representative on the bench, Judge William Clancy, fined a lawyer for contempt of court because the lawyer talked so loud that he broke in on the judge's afternoon nap during a trial, Butte smiled again. Who, after all, had elected Judge Clancy? Butte had.

When Madam Mae Malloy's brothel, the Irish World, opened, its facilities were so impressive that the debut was announced with engraved, R.S.V.P. cards. The less favored girls in the "cribs" on Galena and Mercury Streets paid a rental of five dollars a night to respectable real estate owners, in addition to a city tax of ten dollars a month, and were haled into court every week on grounds of immorality, fined, and released until the next scheduled fine was due. An eminent, if retired, veteran of Galena Street, Nigger Liz, had her place in the Butte scheme of things as a sort of pioneer. Had she not been a prostitute in Alder Gulch, making life more agreeable for other pioneers? She lived to be more than eighty, and, as the local saying went, if the wages of sin is death she waited a long time until payday. In Dublin Gulch, Dan's Hobo Retreat served beef stew free, and whiskey at ten cents a shot, to the down-and-out. Under its granite surface, Butte had a heart tough but warm. . . .

My friend Evan and I stepped off the train at the Northern Pacific station. We arrived in style by taxi at the Thornton Hotel. We dined in leisure at an Italian restaurant in Meaderville, drinking cautiously the Dago Red table wine for which Meaderville was justly famed. Returning from that suburb to the city's center, we entered the Atlantic Bar, which boasted that it contained the longest bar, and the most widely varied gambling appointments, in Montana. The Atlantic was buzzing. The roulette wheels were spinning, the cards were slapping on poker tables. A dozen players were standing around the green-felt craps game layout, above which, in a tall chair, sat a grim-faced "lookout" whose job it was to see that no player placed a bet after the dice were thrown. The player who took such a chance did so at his peril. The "lookout" had a gun in a holster.

We were in fine fettle by now, Evan and I. Perhaps Butte was a shade less rambunctious than it had once been, but we agreed that it would do. Less rambunctious? As we were passing a poker table on our way to a session with the dice, a man sitting opposite the dealer yelped angrily, "You went south for that ace, you son of a bitch!" The dealer had dealt himself an ace from the bottom of the pack. The player who observed this whipped out a gun and shot the dealer through the shoulder. A doctor, but no policeman, was called. The ace dealt from the bottom had been so clumsily apparent that there could be no reason for summoning the law.

Evan and I proceeded to the craps table and took our place in the group surrounding it. We lost. We lost all but five dollars of what remained of the one hundred with which we had so bravely left Missoula that afternoon. The specter of our hotel bill, and our railroad fare back to Missoula, loomed disconcertingly. What, then, to do? A visit to a former *Missoulian* reporter, Bass Yarling, who had moved on to the Butte *Post*, brought a loan of twenty dollars and another chance. The second chance was a lucky one. Holding the dice, Evan hit a streak. In half an hour we had recovered our original capital and more. Weighed down with silver dollars, we repaid the doubtless astonished Mr. Yarling and strolled toward Galena Street.

The ladies of Galena Street, tapping on windows with pennies, solicited attention and announced rates. A number of them were, or seemed to be, very handsome. Faintly red lights shone through ruby-colored transoms.

"This is a good town," said Evan appreciatively as we climbed onto a Northern Pacific train for Missoula on Sunday morning, weary but rich. On a return visit to the Atlantic on Saturday night, his luck with the dice had held. Our one hundred dollars had advanced to three hundred, with all expenses paid.

When I reported to Mr. Ferguson the next morning on some but not all the details of our expedition, he rolled a cigarette and gazed contemplatively, as usual, across the street.

"Before you went to Butte," he said, "I advised you that no one should go there before reaching a certain age. I trust that you reached it safely."

Ghost Town

SPEAKING FOR HIMSELF, said Mr. Ferguson, he had little use for the mining ghost towns. He preferred places where there was someone to talk with and something more interesting to listen to than a hooting owl or a whistling marmot.

"Moreover," he added, "I find ghost towns depressing. Every last one of them smells of failure. No matter how much wealth they turned up for some people, they filled others with ideas that got nowhere. It may be, however, that I am insufficiently romantic. If you insist on going to see what's left of Granite, go right ahead. Try not to fall down one of those deserted tunnels, though, because there might not be anybody around to pull you out. If you get back alive, I'll take a two-thousand-word piece for next Sunday."

It was going to be a fine day, I thought, as I set out at dawn in the Hupmobile, which for all its sturdiness would be put to the test on this expedition. Granite, named for the mine that ranked among the world's richest silver strikes, sat on top of a mountain up which a high-crowned, seldom-used dirt road climbed about two thousand feet in four miles from the town of Philipsburg, its still thriving neighbor. The little Hupmobile had never yet failed, however, nor would it do so now.

So we were in a splendid mood this morning, the Hupmobile and I, as we went east through Hell Gate Canyon,

sliding along the trail the Blackfeet and Flatheads followed
when they raided one another for horses or scalps. The mist
drifted above the shallow, fast-running Clark Fork River.
The motor purred. Indians, missionaries, mule-skinners, gold
miners filled my mind, and suddenly I was in Drummond,
fifty-odd miles from Missoula, where the southbound road
branched off to Philipsburg and Granite, thirty miles away.
I tried to remember, as I came into Philipsburg, what I knew
about its and Granite's history. It was not a great deal. Mr.
Ferguson, who constantly cautioned me—for my own good
and the *Missoulian*'s—to dig into the background of any
story I embarked on, would be disapproving if he were aware
that I had been so casual.

One Hector Horton, I remembered reading somewhere,
had come across a silver lode hereabouts in 1865, and the result was Philipsburg and the claims that developed in the
vicinity, notably one called the Hope. But the Hope apparently was hopeless as early as 1869, and the up-and-com-
ing town of Philipsburg seemed about to expire. It might
have done just that save for an optimist named Eli Holland
who climbed higher up the mountain south of the town and
came upon what was to be the Granite Mountain Mine, a
discovery akin in its silvery way to Tommy Cruse's Drum
Lummon and scarcely less dramatic. Old Eli, the legend
went, shot a deer, watched its hooves kick up what appeared
to be a shower of white sparks, and collected specimens of
the quartz. Assayed, it showed promise. The wonderful
Granite Mountain Mine was on its way, although not at a
rushing pace. A quartz mine in a high, remote place is no
easy operation. Some years later, in 1881, discouraged and
low in funds, Eli was ready to sell to a St. Louis interest represented by Charles D. McClure, a native of the Missouri
frontier, in his teens a freighter and a cattleman, at twenty-
one a shrewd miner who had learned his business alongside
the veterans of Alder Gulch and Last Chance, at thirty-three

the manager of Montana's first mill for the crushing of silver ore, located a block south of Philipsburg's main street. Mr. McClure, whose eye missed very little in its analysis of any rock that promised a reasonable fiscal return, had not overlooked the possibilities in a certain ledge up there on the claim Eli Holland was ready to sell. In one outcropping where others had seen only lowgrade ore the McClure instinct sensed treasure.

All that had been long before the Hupmobile and I pulled into Philipsburg, a lively little place that seemed to hang by its fingertips to its small niche on the Continental Divide's western slope. The streets ran this way and that, up hill and down, following one claim or another: a mining town and no mistaking it. In what other kind of town would the windows of almost every business house offer samples of ore and maps of mines with names like Bay Horse, Shark Town and Scratch All? I wandered around those uneven streets, relishing the bustle and stir of the one-time silver camp that had found another asset—manganese—to keep it alive. I was all but forgetting that my reason for being here this day was the ghost town up on the summit above, the great Granite Mountain Mine. The time was running on. Stopping for lunch in a cafe, I fell into talk with an old man with a scarred face and three fingers missing from his left hand. A veteran miner, almost certainly. The hunch was right. He had known the town of Granite when it flourished? He had. He might be free to drive up the mountain with me this afternoon? He would be.

His name was Dennis McGootry, and he was talking at a rapid rate even before the Hupmobile, puffing but gallant, went up the steep climb.

"You understand, now, there wasn't just the town down in Philipsburg and another one up on the mountain," he said. "It was one town right along the way, cabins, stores, saloons. But when you got to the top, you saw something like you never saw in the gold camps. This was a town that was figured to be around as long as any other town out here, and longer than most. Somehow, in the gold camps, you always reckoned the gold would run out. But the silver that was here, it didn't look like it would ever run out. Of course, that was after Mr. McClure found out what was really in the Granite Mountain Mine."

He spoke of Mr. McClure, I said, the way old copper miners spoke of Marcus Daly—that is, with reverence.

"Why not?" Mr. McGootry snapped. "There were those who allowed he knew all Daly knew about mining, and more. I thought so myself."

Mr. McClure, obviously, had had complete confidence in his own judgment of that certain outcropping overlooked by others. And the St. Louis interests he represented had shared that confidence, at least for a while, long enough to invest $75,000 in developing the Granite Mountain Mine.

"But finally," said Mr. McGootry, "the St. Louis people get tired of paying out and not getting enough back. They wire an order telling Mr. McClure to shut down. He gets the telegram one night when we're working on Tunnel No. Two, and by rights he should have quit when he was told to, but he decides to let us work out the night shift. We put in one last charge, a big one, light the fuse, and get out of the tunnel, and of course you know what happens then."

I knew only vaguely about what happened then.

"We hit it with that last blast," said Mr. McGootry, "The big one, the bonanza. You could see it shining, right there on the planks on the tunnel floor when we go back in. All of a sudden Mr. McClure's a great man, and there's a solid town of three thousand people up there."

Mr. McGootry was dwelling on the glories of that solid town.

"Those gold rush camps, all tents and logs and false fronts. Up here, we had the real thing, an opera house and a miners' hall built of stone, and good little houses where miners lived with their families. For the miners that didn't have families there was a line of girls as good as any in Butte. There was a Chinatown, and half a dozen places to buck the tiger—faro, if you don't know what that means. And that Mr. McClure, he does everything right. The tunnels are dry, and he sets up a hospital, and a library for the boys who can keep away from the girls on the line long enough to read if they know how to read. There's eleven saloons and four churches, not so odd, the way things went then. In winter it gets bad—you come up out of a warm tunnel into zero air, pneumonia can hit you and kill you in two days. But the money is all right, three-fifty for a ten-hour shift, and what's to keep a man from bringing up a few dollars of silver ore in the dinner pail at the end of the day? I think Mr. McClure knew it and didn't mind."

Now we were nearing the top of the mountain, and Mr. McGootry fell into a startling silence, and in a moment I saw why. We reached the crest, and there were the ghostly, bleak remains of Granite. The big mills and furnaces, weather-beaten to a reddish hue, still stood. The huge miners' hall, roofless, dominated the mountaintop and the sky. Chattering birds swooped through its staring windows, but otherwise there was no sound until Mr. McGootry sighed a sigh in memory of departed youth.

"Now you see why it wasn't like Bannack and those places?" he asked. "No flash in the pan here. Folks built homes and brought in furniture like they'd have in Helena and Butte. God knows how all that stuff got freighted up the mountain. They even brought water up here, five gallons a day to a family, a dollar a month. I reckon there was as much whiskey as water, though."

A marmot whistled, and I thought of Mr. Ferguson's distaste for old mining camps and their lost hopes.

At that moment, eerily, Mr. McGootry was saying, "And

then, God damn it, it was all over! In one day, mind you—
one single day—the day in 'ninety-three when the price of
silver went to hell, the order came out from St. Louis to Mr.
McClure to close down, and this time it was for good. I've
been around awhile, and I never saw anything like it, and I
wish I'd never had to see this. Down the mountain, all day
and night, go the miners, some with wives and kids, and the
girls from the line, and the gamblers. They pile into Philipsburg, looking for food and work, and Philipsburg is scared.
The people there, and ranchers around the valley, are carrying guns, and you can't blame 'em. A miner with a hungry
family is apt to get mean. Business houses close down. A
bank busts."

Was it on the very same day, I wondered, that Colonel
Thomas Cruse rode serenely through those Helena crowds
paralyzed and enraged by the Panic of '93? Almost certainly
it was. Suddenly that day was more real to me than this one:
time was playing its odd tricks again, to the point where I
heard myself saying absent-mindedly, "The Colonel had the
right idea about gold. It was sounder than silver."

"The Colonel? Gold?" said Mr. McGootry. He seemed
concerned. "What Colonel? Maybe the altitude's too much
for you, son. Seven thousand feet—it takes some getting used
to. . . . Well," he said, looking over his shoulder at all
that was left of the town in which he had been a young
miner, "I doubt I'll ever be up here again. No point in it.
I'll go fishing down in Flint Creek tomorrow, or over in
Georgetown Lake. Best trout in the State. It's about all I
have to do nowadays."

"You're back alive, I'm glad to see," said Mr. Ferguson the
next morning. "Did you happen to get a story for Sunday?"

"I hope so," I said. "Do you suppose the *Missoulian* could
buy a fancy new fishing rod for Mr. Dennis McGootry of
Philipsburg?"

Mr. Ferguson rolled a cigarette while he gazed at me inquiringly. "Mr. McGootry? A fishing rod? I was afraid of what one of those crazy ghost towns might do to you. Maybe it was the altitude up there at Granite. Give yourself an hour to get over it, and then drop around to the courthouse and see how many people are suing other people."

XXI

Heroes' Reward

THE FASCINATION THAT THE CIVIL WAR HELD for a romantically inclined reporter scarcely out of his teens by turns perplexed and amused Mr. Ferguson.

"Has it ever occurred to you," he asked me one day, "how much of the West was settled by people who were running away from that war?"

I pointed out to him, with some heat, that among the old gentlemen to whom, when I was a boy, I listened on long summer afternoons were veterans of Gettysburg, Antietam, Shiloh.

With only the slightest of smiles, Mr. Ferguson let the "when I was a boy" go unremarked and returned to his point. He was not, he said, speaking of those noble heroes of mine.

"What I'm talking about," he said, "are all those thousands of husky young men in Bannack and Alder Gulch back there in 'sixty-two through 'sixty-five. They must have been in pretty good shape, or they couldn't have dug for gold twelve hours a day. Why weren't they soldiering with Grant and Sherman or, for that matter, Lee and Jackson?"

A lot of them, I submitted, came from the Border States and chose to go West because of divided loyalties.

"*Some* of them," said Mr. Ferguson, with a note of correction. "At the risk of disillusionment, I could direct your attention to a good many more of the builders of our great

185

State—copper kings, cattlemen and others—who avoided the war for a couple of simple reasons. They didn't like the idea of getting killed, and they wanted to make money while someone else was preserving or trying to destroy the Union.

"That being the case," he continued, "I venture to suggest that you go to see a couple of men who fought through the war and then came out here, but arrived too late. It might be a saddening experience, but it could teach you something."

And who, I inquired, were these luckless veterans?

"One of them," he said, "is Peter Perry, and you will find him in Mr. Justice of the Peace A. J. Hutton's court today as a defendant. The other is Stephen Dukes, and you will find him any day at all at the county farm." (This was the local euphemism for "county poorhouse.") "Long live the Republic," said Mr. Ferguson with a ferocity unusual in him.

All I knew about Peter Perry was that he was a long-standing nuisance to the Northern Pacific Railway, whose tracks adjoined his 160 acres near the crest of Evaro Hill twelve miles to the northwest. A few clippings in the morgue told me a little more, but not much, about him. Anyhow, it was time to be getting over to the courthouse and Justice Hutton's court, where justice was dispensed with an informality that would have startled Chief Justice William Howard Taft of the United States Supreme Court back in Washington, D.C.

The case was about to open. The defendant was sitting beside a kitchen table with his court-appointed attorney, a young man recently graduated from the University of Montana Law School. The defendant's face was largely covered by snowy whiskers from which two watery blue eyes gleamed with something like venom. He might have been eighty or ninety or a hundred. At another table sat the Northern Pacific's slick-haired attorney, with a patronizing smile and a confident air, not less confident because Justice Hutton himself was an old N.P. man and presumably sympathetic to the cause of his former employer.

Justice Hutton wheezed, adjusted the vest over his large stomach, and called the court to order. He read the charge. Peter Perry, the plaintiff complained, did maliciously and with malice aforethought and danger to the public weal, etc., roll logs onto the tracks of the Northern Pacific. He had done this before, but recently he had added a new offense. He had set up a barricade, designed to be a toll house, and proposed to levy a fee of one hundred dollars on every train coming through, with an additional charge if the train was the railroad's pride, the *North Coast Limited*. There was laughter in the court. How did he plead, guilty or not guilty?

With surprising agility Peter leaped to his feet. "The sons of bitches!" he shouted in a voice that shook the windows in Justice Hutton's court. "It's my land they're on! Not guilty!"

"Take it easy," said the Justice. "Sit down."

"The hell I will," said Peter. "I was with Farragut at Mobile Bay in 'sixty-four. I was at the bow gun on Farragut's *Hartford* when we rammed the *Tennessee*. Where were you?"

"I wasn't born yet," the Justice said, with a sigh, and called on the plaintiff's attorney to bring on his first witness. The witness, the engineer of the *North Coast Limited*, testified that if he had not been moving down the steep Evaro grade with extreme caution there certainly would have been a wreck. The second witness, chief conductor of the *North Coast Limited* and therefore a figure of awe in a railroad-minded community, testified that an hour of the *North Coast Limited*'s valuable time had been consumed before the toll house barricade could be removed.

"It's my land!" Peter shouted again.

"*Your* land?" said the Northern Pacific attorney. "Who says so?"

"I say so, you bastard!" Peter yelled. It was an old sailor's voice, all right, one to be heard above wind and storm.

"Shut up, Peter," said the Justice.

The Northern Pacific attorney ran on. Who was this

demented octogenarian, he demanded, to think he could threaten the lives of five hundred people on a Seattle-to-Chicago train? The attorney asked that Peter be put away for an indefinite period and his 160 acres placed under the jurisdiction of the court, all this out of concern for the public interest. Justice Hutton reserved judgment on this point. What, in the meantime, was the case for the defense? Peter's attorney rose, without obvious enthusiasm for the task he faced. He was clearly about to put in a plea for merciful consideration by the court.

He was scarcely under way before he was cut down by the voice of his client.

"God damn you all!" Peter roared. "I got this land instead of a pension after the war. It's a land patent. I got the papers to prove it."

Why then, the Northern Pacific attorney asked, had he been so long in defending his claim? Because, said Peter—who had now fully taken over his own defense—he had been away for quite a spell when the Northern Pacific was coming through in the early '80's. He had returned to the Navy, and served hitches in the merchant marine of one country and another, and gone gold-hunting in the Yukon, and by the time he finally came home he found railroad tracks across his land.

"By right of eminent domain," said the Northern Pacific attorney.

"What's that?" Peter wanted to know. "And none of your Goddamn fancy language."

"Order in the court," said Justice Hutton. "Eminent domain," he explained, "is when the government says it can take whatever it needs to take."

"The government?" Peter was all but screaming now. "If it was the Rebs that won the war, they could sure take it. They'd have had the say. But we won it, Admiral Farragut and us. God damn it, don't you sit there and tell me the

188

government gives me a piece of land for fightin' and then turns around and gives it to a Goddamn railroad!"

"The government didn't have no choice, Peter," said Justice Hutton. "The railroad had to build over your land. There wasn't no other pass in the northern Bitter Roots. They'd have had to go a hundred miles south."

"Why the hell didn't they?" Peter asked.

"I don't know," said Justice Hutton, "but I guess you'd better cool off awhile, maybe thirty days down here with the sheriff. We'll fix you up comfortable, and I'll see your place gets taken care of and the dog and chickens fed."

"And let the Goddamn railroad keep going right through my place, is that it?" Peter cried.

But then he calmed down suddenly, and to the mild embarrassment of everyone, including even the Northern Pacific attorney, his voice dropped to a level just above tears.

"Hell of a thing," he said, "to happen to a man that was with Farragut at Mobile Bay. We won the war for you bastards sitting on your backsides here. He'd damn you to the fire for what you're doing to one of his boys."

"I'm sorry, Peter," said Justice Hutton. "I sure am."

"You oughta be," said Peter.

When I reported the morning's events to Mr. Ferguson, he said only, "Now that you have observed one hero's reward, you might go up and see Mr. Dukes at the county farm. I hear that he has been waiting only sixty years for something to be done about his pension. It might put him in a better frame of mind if you took along some of that moonshine rot-gut your generation calls whiskey."

How Mr. Ferguson had come to know about Stephen Dukes I did not inquire, perhaps because it did not seem necessary. I took it for granted that Mr. Ferguson, like my father, knew everything. Certainly Mr. Ferguson was right, as usual, in his surmise about the moonshine. Mr. Dukes, sitting on a log outside his tent at the county farm, took a large, appreciative gulp straight from the bottle. With a knife that he might have carried into battle three score years before, he cut a large slice from a plug of chewing tobacco. He gazed contentedly at the sunset's glow on Mount Jumbo, Mount Sentinel's companion on the north side of the Clark Fork River, and spat a long stream in its direction. He was a gaunt specter of a man, with a handlebar moustache, a sparse set of chin whiskers, a scratchy voice.

"What do you want to know?" he asked.

I said I had been told that he never had received the pension he should have had for his Civil War service, and why was that?

"Oh, Jesus," said Mr. Dukes, in the resigned manner of one who had told the story often but was not averse to telling it again.

At seventeen he had enlisted in the Fifty-fifth Illinois and, he said, served with "Uncle Billy"—Gen. William Tecumseh Sherman—from Shiloh to the Battle of Atlanta.

"Vicksburg, Kenesaw Mountain. Where didn't we go?" Mr. Dukes said. "But the best was right before Atlanta, the Allatoona Hills and New Hope Church and them places."

"The best?" I asked.

"Yep," said Mr. Dukes, "I liked the shootin' and the excitement. Uncle Billy himself pulls a sliver out of my throat from the canister Hood's Texans was throwin' at us at New Hope. He sticks me in the rear with it and says, 'You ain't hurt. Get up and fight.' I was fixin' to anyhow."

To Mr. Dukes' intense annoyance, when Sherman left Atlanta for the sea, he left young Stephen behind as an orderly serving General George H. Thomas. When the war ended less than a year later, he went to the Mexican border with General Phil Sheridan and 50,000 troops, mostly cavalry, to keep an eye on the Archduke Maximilian of Austria, Napoleon III's puppet emperor in the New World.

"But they wasn't nobody to fight," said Mr. Dukes, "so General Sheridan tells me to go on home, because I wasn't any sort of cavalryman anyhow. Well, now, it was hard to get back in them days. No boats out of Galveston for a long time. By the time I get back to Springfield, Illinois, my old regiment is mustered out, and I have hell's own time proving I wasn't a deserter, but finally it gets cleared up and I get my papers. I save 'em until a dozen years ago, when I need money, and send 'em to the Congressman from my old district in Illinois—Representative Halliday, Vermilion County. He don't answer. I write to President Harding, and he writes a real nice letter saying it'll all get fixed up, providing I find two survivors from the old Fifty-fifth who'll say I served all right. Would you believe it? There ain't two survivors that anybody can find. Maybe it ain't so strange at that. Half the regiment died in the war."

Mr. Dukes emitted a stream of tobacco juice that surprised a squirrel at twenty feet and said he had made one half-hearted appeal for a pension some years before.

"Could have had it, too. But there I was, freightin' between Idaho and the Blackfoot Valley up here, and they wanted me to go all the way to Salt Lake City for an examination. Salt Lake, mind you, when I had eight mules to look after. How could I go?"

Did he ever regret, I wondered—I was thinking of Mr. Ferguson—that he had enlisted in '61 instead of heading off to the West to make his fortune and leave the preservation of the Union to someone else?

Mr. Dukes was surprised. "Think what I'd have missed!" he said. "Watchin' General Grant set on his horse at Shiloh, calm as you please, and Uncle Billy takin' a sliver out of my rear with his own hands. No, I ain't sorry."

The sun was now almost down, and Mr. Dukes' ebullience dropped with it.

"Still and all," he was saying, "I wonder what I'd have

thought then if somebody'd told me I'd be winding up in a poorhouse."

But when I asked him if I could come back another day, he perked up.

"Any time," he said. "When anybody's in a place like this, you know damn well he's got more time than money."

"Well," said Mr. Ferguson when I came back to the office, "I trust that Mr. Dukes cured you of some of your romantic notions about the Civil War."

"Mr. Dukes enjoyed the war," I said.

"You are hopeless," said Mr. Ferguson. "You, and Mr. Dukes, too."

XXII

Mr. Callahan

Now it was 1926, and, direct from commencement at an Eastern college, I reported to Mr. Ferguson at the *Missoulian-Sentinel* office. As I climbed those steep stairs leading up from West Main Street, I had a fine feeling of homecoming—the musty smell of tobacco, the sharp fragrance of ink, the smoke-stained walls, the old friends in the city room—but I was aware also of a subtle difference.

The summer vacation jobs had been instructive and happy. From now on, however, life would be serious. There was a craft to be learned, if I was to be a full-time newspaperman. The first stages of my further education had been placed by my father in the hands of his managing editor. There would be no suspicion of favoritism, if my father could help it, and he obviously could.

At 7:55 A.M. Mr. Ferguson was pouring tobacco into a straw-colored cigarette paper. His gold-rimmed glasses shone beneath his green eyeshade. His voice was as cheerfully ironic as ever.

I was quite sure, he inquired, that I wanted to make a career of this profession? I was. Mr. Ferguson allowed himself his first aphorism of the day.

"There is no other business in which a person can have so much fun for so little money," he said.

He had been pondering the schedule I would follow. It

would begin at 8 A.M. with two hours of re-writing and bringing up to date stories from the morning *Missoulian* for the evening *Sentinel*. From 10 A.M. to 4 P.M. I would cover the city hall (police, health department, mayor's office) and the county courthouse (sheriff's and county attorney's offices, two county judges, assessor's office, clerk of the court). From 4 P.M. to 6 P.M. I would be on call for odd jobs that Mr. Ferguson did not doubt he could provide. I would be ready to do whatever I was asked to do by my elders and betters, Mr. Rocene, Mr. Rosendorf, Mr. Swartz, Mr. Hutchens (a slight smile here) and himself.

"You will be lied to by almost all elected officials," said Mr. Ferguson, "and you will learn to know when you are lied to. You will also learn that a politician is a man who practices the art of politics at its most realistic level—that is to say, the art of getting into office and, if possible, remaining there. You will come to know that an officer of the law more often than not is a plumber who is legally entitled to wear a star and carry a gun." He reflected for a moment. He added, "I will cite one exception on your beat. He is Deputy Sheriff Pat Callahan."

And so, on that very first day as a would-be full-time newspaperman, I met Pat Callahan.

Who, in Missoula, had not heard something of the Callahan story, or at least had not seen him at a distance, the Irishman built like a pile-driving fullback, the huge hands, the placid face (a bit like that of the cartoon character Jiggs), the deliberate gait? Heeding Mr. Ferguson's words, I tried to recall what more I knew about him and came up with nothing much except a legend about a former saloon keeper who, singlehanded, subdued the toughest Montana town within recent memory. But it was not, as I was to discover, a legend. It was a fact.

Mr. Callahan—he was always to be "Mr. Callahan" to me—was lolling on a bench in the sheriff's office when I arrived there in mid-afternoon of this hot June day. I introduced myself. He extended a huge paw and with the other put down a copy of what, it transpired, was his favorite book, *The Orations of Thomas Francis Meagher*, the Irish patriot, leader of the Irish Brigade in the American Civil War, Acting Governor of Montana Territory. In a soft-voiced brogue Mr. Callahan wished me well in my new duties. We would become better acquainted as time went on, he trusted. We would indeed become better acquainted, to the point where a young reporter's proudest claim was that he was a friend of Mr. Callahan and had heard the Callahan story from Mr. Callahan himself, bit by bit, in that office.

It was a story that began in the 1870's with his birth in County Mayo, whence his mother and stepfather emigrated to Canada in 1885, leaving the young Patrick to fend for himself as a groom and virtual peon on a big estate until he escaped into a bog and was kept alive by an Irish wolfhound that fetched him rabbits. And the story went on to say how, with a little money sent by his mother in Canada, he went by steerage to the New World, so green that he neglected to take his own food for the passage and all but starved; and how, arriving in Toronto, he found his mother the frequently beaten victim of her brutal husband, whom the young Patrick thrashed until he feared he had killed him, then hurried into western Canada to hide out from the law—as he supposed he had to—in railroad construction and lumber camps.

He was a rugged lad, nearing twenty, when he slid out from under a freight train in Missoula and went to church for the first time in some months. Had anyone in the congregation, the priest asked from the altar, heard of the whereabouts of a young man named Pat Callahan? Surely the law was closing in on him now, young Patrick thought, and went to the priest after Mass to give himself up for the murder of his stepfather. But no, the message was from his mother, saying that he had merely broken a few of the stepfather's bones and taught him a lesson.

The years went by quickly and well enough. Mr. Callahan was a man of parts, and much respected: the family man who rejoiced in his wife and three children, the saloon keeper who did not drink, the renowned rough-and-tumble fighter who never started a fight but inevitably finished one. In Mr. Callahan's Montana Saloon on Railroad Avenue the very awareness of the Callahan fists was enough to preserve order. Lumberjacks coming into town from the spring log drives in the Blackfoot Valley occasionally challenged his reputation as champion of the no-holds-barred brawl. (A derogatory word about the Pope was the preferred opening gambit.) No challenger ever was known to repeat the challenge. The rough-necks went away calling his place, somewhat bitterly, "a parlor saloon," too quiet to be enjoyable.

Then it was 1909, and the Chicago, Milwaukee and St. Paul Railroad was pushing toward the West Coast. At Taft, in Western Montana, the line's extension was stalled by the prolonged cutting of a tunnel through the Rockies. A railroad construction town grew up, a ferocious one populated by whores, pimps, tin-horn gamblers, and some hundreds of hard-rock, hard-muscled, working stiffs. The murder rate in Taft was averaging one a week when the railroad called on the sheriff of Missoula County for help.

"Get Pat Callahan," said the Missoula sheriff.

The dignified, saloon-keeping Mr. Callahan was officially deputized. He put on his best suit and his iron hat, packed a few belongings in his cardboard suitcase, and took the train for Taft, the turbulent town inappropriately named for the easygoing incumbent President of the United States.

Mr. Callahan's reputation as a mighty man with his hands had preceded him. On the platform at Taft, as the train came in, was a welcoming committee of six local sluggers. Mr. Callahan stepped down from the train, took in the nature of the

196

reception, put down his suitcase, placed his iron hat on it, walked up to the largest and ruggedest of the group, hurled a right fist at his chin, and stepped back. The man he had hit dropped as if axed.

"Anybody else?" Mr. Callahan asked mildly.

These were the first words spoken. The circle dissolved.

He picked up his suitcase, walked down the town's single street to what passed for a hotel, and that evening announced some rules.

The pimps and gamblers were given two hours to get out of town. The girls could stay. Mr. Callahan, family man and churchgoer though he was, recognized certain basic facts of life and their place in the frontier's social scheme. Fist fights were to be permitted between evenly matched battlers who insisted on battle, but there was to be no bullying. Anyone shooting save in self-defense might find himself shot by Mr. Callahan.

All was not immediately serene in Taft. A railroad foreman who refused to turn over his crew's wages to their Rumanian gypsy tribal chief, to be distributed after the chief had taken his cut, was beaten to death by the gypsy's bodyguard. Mr. Callahan, with the whole town watching him, took action. Sauntering into the saloon where the killers waited confidently, he floored the chief with a swipe of his broad left hand and covered the bodyguard with a Colt six-gun held in his right. He marched the whole company, bodyguard and chief, off to the local jail to be dispatched to Missoula for trial. Not a shot had been fired.

As the tunnel neared completion, order had reigned in Taft for six months, though not without some frays. Mr. Callahan's total of knockouts reached thirty or forty. He shot the gun out of one would-be killer's hand. His mission accomplished, he boarded the train for Missoula, with his iron hat and his cardboard suitcase, pausing only to announce that any violation of his rules would bring his immediate return.

Taft knew he meant it. Neither the pimps nor the tin-horn gamblers came back. No further death by violence occurred.

With national Prohibition, Mr. Callahan's saloon shut down and he became a deputy sheriff in Missoula. His Taft record remained a living force. Riots, strikes, street brawls—whatever the difficulty, someone would say, "Here comes Callahan," and trouble melted.

He was getting on in years when I met him—that is, he was a bit over fifty—but one would hardly have taken an oath on it. Walking to work across the Higgins Avenue bridge one chill spring morning, not long after sunrise, I glanced down into the river and saw what appeared to be a white porpoise thrashing through the swift current toward a small, shivering dog on a rock in midstream. Mr. Callahan, stripped to his shorts, rose out of the water, took the dog under one arm, and thrashed his way back to the north bank where a small boy stood waiting and crying. Dog and boy disappeared on the run. Mr. Callahan moved behind a bush to put on the rest of his clothes. Later that day I gave him to understand that I had seen all, and that it would make an affecting story for the paper.

"Ye'll be writing nothing about it," he said. His light blue eyes were genial as always, but his tone was firm. The story was not written.

Another story went unwritten, although in this case Mr. Callahan did not insist. He merely suggested. A local businessman and his wife, both young, had quarreled violently and drunkenly. The wife, through a locked bedroom door, announced her impending suicide. The husband phoned Mr. Callahan. Mr. Callahan arrived, placed his shoulder to the door and opened it, and took a bullet through a coat sleeve, close enough to singe his arm, before he disarmed the wife. Characteristically, although shot at, he chose to take no further action. Even so, it seemed to me a good story, even if written "blind," without names.

"Think, now," said Mr. Callahan. "There's a little piece for the paper, but everybody in the neighborhood knows who ye're talking about, and they slice the story out of the paper and save it, and a long time later this lady's kids read it, and they know who it's about. It hurts them more than it interests anybody today. Is it worth it to ye, now, and honestly?"

I guessed maybe it wasn't and thus learned something about a sense of proportion, although Mr. Callahan would not have called it anything so fancy, and, I feared, Mr. Ferguson or my father would have called it something quite different and harsher if they were to discover my departure from the stern code of news gathering.

The last time I saw Mr. Callahan was during my final week as a resident Montanan. It was on a night in 1927 outside a public dance at the county fairgrounds where the moonshine whiskey was flowing. A tough youngster who had done some professional prize fighting was on the way to making trouble. The big right hand of Mr. Callahan descended on his shoulder —the hand of which someone has said that, if it kept on pushing, a man would disappear right into the ground.

"That'll be enough," said Mr. Callahan.

"Take off that star and hand over that gun to somebody, and I'll lick you," said the tough young man.

Mr. Callahan did neither. The bystanders murmured. This was not like him.

"That's enough," he said. "Go home."

The young man spat in the dirt, close to the Callahan shoes. Mr. Callahan merely blinked. The murmurs increased. Was he really, at last, too old? Had he gone soft? The young man spat again.

Mr. Callahan drew a long breath, as of resignation to a step to be taken more in sorrow than in anger. He took off the star, unloaded the gun, handed it to someone standing next to him, and waited. The young man rushed him, ducked under a Callahan punch, and kneed him in the groin. Mr.

Callahan winced, grunted, turned, and caught him with the famous Callahan right to the ear. The young man dropped. By all the accepted rules of rough-and-tumble combat, that kneeing in the groin entitled Mr. Callahan—in the local phrase—to "put the boots" to him. He did not. He sat down slowly, weightily, on his enemy's stomach.

The crowd's laughter was a happy, cleansing roar in the night. Maybe the old man wasn't what he had been at Taft, but he still had it. Civic pride surrounded him.

Mr. Callahan looked around at his appreciative audience. Those blue Irish eyes fixed on me. "I must be gettin' on, son," he said. "When I knock 'em down now, I don't want to let 'em get up. So ye're goin' east soon to work for one of those New York papers? Take care of yourself."

I didn't trust myself to speak. I shook that mighty right hand for the last time. I really knew, then, what Mr. Ferguson meant when he had said, "I will cite one exception, Deputy Sheriff Pat Callahan. . . ."

When I told Mr. Ferguson the next morning about the incident of the evening before, he added a note to the Callahan canon.

"Do you happen to know," he observed, "that Mr. Callahan never killed a man in his life? He never had to. *That's* being tough."

XXIII

Charlie Russell

I SAW HIM ONLY ONCE, at his summer studio at the foot of Lake McDonald in West Glacier Park, the finest of all artists of the American Old West, Charles Marion Russell: a stocky, broad-shouldered man, neither tall nor short, with the rugged, lined, weather-beaten face—and the Stetson hat—of the cowboy he had been. His jaw was square and prominent, his eyes gray and deep-set, his dignity Indian-like. His hat well back on his head, he sat before his easel that day, working, while a drove of Montana State Press Association members visited his studio as a feature of their annual state convention. I do not recall why he happened to let himself in for such an invasion as this, but he was laconically polite and went on painting. He doubtless had a few old acquaintances among the visiting journalists, but no one could have been less interested than he in what they might write about him when they went home to their offices. By this time—1924— his art, as painter and sculptor, was internationally recognized. His indifference to fame, flattery and money was exactly as it had been when he came into Great Falls in 1892 from the open range, a cowboy who had to paint.

Save among friends of his early days, and those whom he later met and with whom he instinctively felt a kinship, he was something of a "loner," said those who knew him best; genial and gregarious when he chose to be, but still a loner.

In any case, he was our—Montana's—Charlie Russell, "the cowboy artist," and our pride in him was and is great, because he belonged [and belongs] to the world as well. Looking back, I can imagine that our Chamber of Commerce "boosters," advocates of a new, shiny, "progressive," urbanized Montana, must have had their doubts about him even while they valued his name. ("Come out and see the Charlie Russell country!") For Charlie Russell loathed "progress," and that was that. He despised automobiles, reformers, barbed wire fences, dry-land farmers who turned the range grass upside down, and "bigness" in any form except the sweep of the great plains all the way to the horizon. Even in the frontier society to which he came as a sixteen-year-old from St. Louis in 1880, he stood somewhat apart. When the only good Indian was held to be a dead Indian, young Charlie liked and understood Indians. In 1888 he lived for six months in Canada among the Bloods, a Blackfoot tribe, learned their sign language, listened to their legends, and in his art portrayed them —as he did all Indians—with an absolute fidelity that won their friendship and respect. As a tow-headed youngster new to the frontier, trying to look as tough as his elders on the range, he carried a gun and pretended to be a hunter. But it simply wasn't in him to kill. He cherished life and hated the infliction of pain. There came a time when he declined even to go fishing.

"But a fish doesn't feel pain," someone said to him.

"He doesn't?" Charlie said sardonically. "That's why he jumps six feet out of the water when he gets a barb in his eye. And the live-bait minnow, wiggling on the hook, he wiggles because it tickles him."

Long before biographers and art critics took him up, Montanans had their Charlie Russell, seeing him not as he saw himself—he was too modest for that—but as strangers could not see him. Who could really appreciate all of Russell until he knew something of the Russell country, the Russell background, the world of horses and plains, red and white men that he recorded in pen and pencil, watercolor, oils and bronze?

Old-timers loitering away the days at the Mint Saloon, his favorite haunt in Great Falls, never tired of talking about him, before his death in 1926 and long after. To some of the more venerable ones he was still "Kid" Russell, the Missouri boy who arrived in Helena by stagecoach, sitting up beside the driver so that his wide eyes would miss nothing, a bit disappointed at first that the Indians he saw were not as Ned Buntline's dime novels pictured them, but prophetically certain that this would be his country, his home. Back in St. Louis, his family was prosperous and distinguished for mercantile enterprise for which his father had thought to groom him. If young Charlie recognized any family influence, though, it was the tradition of his great-uncle, William Bent, fur trader and explorer, builder of the trading post renowned throughout the West as Bent's Fort, in what came to be Colorado. A boy with the Bent blood in him had small time for school or for anything else in St. Louis but lingering on the waterfront, watching the Missouri River steamboats setting out for faraway Fort Benton, at the navigable head of Old Muddy, carrying household goods and machinery, returning with gold and travelers' tales. That, and the pictures he was always drawing, the objects he was incessantly modeling in clay or wax.

Perhaps, his family thought, a New Jersey military school's discipline would be the answer. A single term proved it was not. Or if he had to be an artist, the family said, let him go to a proper art school in St. Louis. He attended such a school for three days and never took another lesson. Clearly he would be restless until he saw that Far West of which he never stopped dreaming and talking, and so the elder Russell arrived at what he deemed a sure-fire solution: Charlie could go to Montana with a family friend who owned a sheep ranch in the Judith Basin. Such a visit should get the West out of the boy's system, so that he would be content to come home to stay.

Insofar as Charlie could not put up with the sheep ranch or its owner, the elder Russell's scheme succeeded. But neither did Charlie go home to stay, then or ever. On his very first day on his own, a hungry, lonesome kid making a cold camp by the Judith River, he fell in with Jake Hoover, mountain man, hunter and trapper, for the next two years his invaluable instructor in the ways of nature, and his great-hearted, life-time friend. For what he learned from Hoover, and for the role this learning played in his art, Russell's gratitude was end-less. The gratitude of Russell's admirers can scarcely be less.

Here, finally, was the life he had yearned for, big country, many animals, few people. Two years later he was night-herding cattle for a Judith Basin outfit, not a top hand but a responsible wrangler, a lively storyteller and popular with his mates in the bunkhouse for a gift he had for quickly and amusingly drawn sketches and caricatures of the life they shared. He was now on the very edge of fame.

He reached it one night early in 1887 when the most fear-ful blizzard in the Territory's history howled around the O H Ranch, in the Basin, where Charlie was wintering. For three days the snow fell steadily and the thermometer hovered at sixty below zero. A chinook (warm wind causing a sudden thaw) was followed by another storm. Frozen cowboys, lashed to their horses, were carried back dead to their ranches. To the owner of the O H came a message from a fellow cattleman in Helena asking how the herds were doing.

"I'll have to write him a letter," said the owner.

"I'll make a sketch to go with it," said Charlie, and dashed off a postcard-sized watercolor of a starved cow about to drop into the snow while the circling wolves watched. "Wait-ing for a Chinook," he labeled it, later adding the title by which it was to become best known: "The Last of 5000."

The owner looked at the picture. "Hell, he don't need a letter. This'll do it."

It did. It also took Charlie Russell's name throughout the cattleman's world, and beyond. But nothing could change him essentially. He had his half year with the Bloods in Canada. As early as 1889 he felt civilization—"progress"—closing in on him in the Judith Basin, and, packing his cheap paints in a sock, with the "brushes" that were the chewed ends of matches and twigs, he rode his pinto horse up to the Milk River. Already he must have sensed that this land he loved was at a transitional point between old and new, that he must capture it on canvas and paper while he could, with all the exactness of which he was capable: cowboys and cow towns, mule skinners, trail bosses, Indians, roundups.

His reputation was spreading beyond Montana's borders, although he seemed unaware of it and thought himself lucky to sell a picture for five or ten dollars in a saloon. When a Great Falls bartender offered him seventy-five dollars a month "and grub" for everything he painted, drew and modeled during a year, the forty-dollar-a-month cowboy was tempted. He discovered that the contract called on him to paint, draw or model daily from 8:00 A.M. to 6:00 P.M. He retreated to Milk River and the range. When he returned to Great Falls the next year, in 1892, he had left the range for good. He would paint, and for himself only.

To the end of his life he called himself not an artist but an "illustrator," and he must have meant it, because he was not given to false humility. What mattered, of course, was that he *was* an artist. The first years in Great Falls when the former cowboy was exclusively an artist were lean. In this period he did some of his finest work, for rewards so slight that he barely made a living. Sometimes he gave it away, as he had given prettily decorated little sugar scoops to the professional girls in the parlor houses in the cow towns of his earlier years. (As late as the 1920's one or another of the "girls," transformed with time into a respectable matron, would bring a sugar scoop to his studio to be touched up. The lady to whom by that time he was married was said to be not entirely pleased by this.) At the Mint Saloon, owned by his friend Sid Willis, he paid for his food and drink with paintings that one day would sell for thousands of dollars. His purity being of a special sort, money meant little to him.

Fortunately for him, it meant more to the woman he married, Miss Nancy Cooper, of Mansfield, Kentucky. Had she not been visiting his old friends, Mr. and Mrs. Ben Roberts, of Cascade, a town south of Great Falls, would the Russell career have taken the turn it did? She was younger than he by fourteen years. She was hard-headed and aggressive as he could never bring himself to be, and the thirty years of their marriage appeared to be happy.

"How much is this picture worth?" a prospective customer asked Charlie in New York, where Nancy and he had gone to investigate the market. "One hundred and fifty dollars," said Charlie. "Eight hundred dollars," said Nancy. The prospective customer paid eight hundred dollars, prompting Charlie to say later, "I'll do the work from now on—you do the selling." She did so, with golden results. One of the last of his pictures sold during his lifetime brought thirty thousand dollars. "Why, that's dead man's prices!" said the astounded Charlie. Very likely he would have been satisfied with three hundred dollars, but that was not the point of Nancy's shrewd bargaining. The point was that her gift for the market place set him free, and he loved freedom.

At about the time he gave up bachelorhood, his pals around the Mint Saloon observed, he cut down on his drinking. A few years later, he gave it up entirely. It had not been a vice with him, and while his friend Will Rogers once made a joke of it—Nancy took an extra "o" out of "saloon" and made it "salon," Rogers said—the old pals did not regard him as unduly corralled. They still had his good company through the

long nights of storytelling at the Mint. The least art-con-
scious of them were aware that he was working through the
day in his log cabin studio on Fourth Avenue North, and
probably working the better for his abstinence.

No, he did not change. In his Stetson, his high-heeled cowboy boots, his crimson Red River sash, he was at home any-
where, in New York and London "art circles" as on Central
Avenue, Great Falls. Animals as well as people seemed to
recognize his unvarying self. On a visit to the St. Louis
World's Fair in 1903, he said his happiest moment was when
he passed a caged coyote and "it licked my hand like he knew
me. I guess I brought the smell of plains with me." His cowboy friend Con Price, perhaps the closest of all his friends,
was to recall a day when he accompanied Russell around
Great Falls while Charlie circulated a petition for the release
from the state penitentiary of an ex-rustler with whom Russell had ridden the range. A righteous citizen declined to sign
the pardon plea. Con Price went on to say:

"I have never forgottten what Charlie said when we left
this fellow. He said justice was the hardest, cruelest word that
ever was written. He said if all the people that were crying
for real justice got it, they would think they were terribly
abused and would not want it and would find out what they
wanted was a little mercy instead."

In a man less complex than Russell, his aversion to change
—change for the worse, as he saw it—might have seemed
merely eccentric. In the art of Charlie Russell, it was a passionate and positive force. Damn the homesteaders' barbed
wire that destroyed a way of life worth saving!—it ran
through his conversation and letters like a recurrent chant.
Persuaded by his wife to address an assembly of Forward
Looking Citizens, he startled them with:

"I have been called a pioneer. In my book a pioneer is a
man who comes to a virgin country, traps off all the fur, kills
off all the wild meat, cuts down all the trees, grazes off all

the grass, plows the roots up, and strings ten million miles of wire. A pioneer destroys things and calls it civilization. I wish to God that this country was just like it was when I first saw it and that none of you folks were here at all."

He strode from the platform, leaving his audience irritated but not, presumably, puzzled—not if it recalled the depth of feeling with which he evoked the past in "When Wagon Trails Were Dim," the sheer exuberance with which he caught the cowboy's hell-raising life in "Smoke of a .45." Action, frequently violent, was the stamp of his early work, and it never ceased to be a major element of his art. "Everything Russ paints is agoin' some," said one of those old fellow cowpunchers who were his favorite critics. But his very greatest pictures, made in his artistic maturity, have about them the eloquence of silence: Indians facing the sunset in "Trail's End" (a title with an added, inadvertent meaning, because it was his very last painting); a man sitting motionless on a horse and looking back at his outfit on a distant trail in "The Wagon Boss." Everywhere Russell's unspoken statement is: "This is the way it was, and was life not better then than now?" Perhaps it was not, to the degree that he believed it to be, but of his passionate conviction there could be no doubt; with the sense of urgency instilled in him by the quickening pace of change, it was a well-spring of his art. "Thank God I was here first," he used to say.

A realist literally to his fingertips, openly scorning impressionism, he nevertheless emphasized light more than composition in his later work, and mood over story and action. The bold early colors gave way to cool serene ones. As the years went by, in still another medium—sculpture—he may have been an even greater artist. The nature of the form being what it is, his bronzes were and still are less well-known than his paintings, although he cast his first piece in bronze as early as 1904. But the boys on the range and around the Mint could not have been astonished at this further sign of his genius. They remembered how "Kid" Russell was forever molding a handful of beeswax or tallow into an animal or a cowboy or an Indian, accurate in detail like everything he did, sometimes keeping it out of sight in his pocket while his long, thin fingers worked, producing it for their admiring attention, then flattening it out and going on to make another. Grown older, the one-time "Kid" shaped clay into permanent form with the superb confidence with which he handled a brush and in the same veins of drama, humor, pathos: a bucking bronc reaching for the sky, a grizzly leading her cubs across a log, Indian hunters riding down a buffalo herd, Sioux and Blackfeet in battle.

If Charlie had been a really accomplished cowboy, some Montanans used to say, he might have been too busy to become an artist, a doubtful supposition in the case of one with the true artist's unconquerable passion to portray and interpret. But it does seem safe to believe that if he had been formally educated and bookish, he would not have been the writer he was—how extraordinary a writer, and how much more than a yarn-spinner and a humorist, I suspect we did not fully appreciate at the time. He was our Charlie Russell, and we took it for granted that he could do splendidly whatever he turned his hand to.

We laughed, as of course he intended us to, at the tall tales in *Rawhide Rawlins*, his first book, and *More Rawhides*, those tales that moved Will Rogers, who heard them told in person, to place his friend Charlie among the greatest of American storytellers. But suddenly, among the comical sketches of cowboys on a tear and flat-bottomed steamboats running up a dry gulch, there would be a somber, haunting one like "Longrope's Last Guard," than which Western American literature offers no more graphic memory of a herd of cattle stampeding at night. Here, in a few hundred words, is something like a definitive portrait of men who daily dealt in danger, buried the unlucky dead, and moved on. For if Russell declared that writing was an effort amounting to agony, what he did write has the easy touch of a man talking to his friends, as in fact he was talking in the letters collected by his widow under the title *Good Medicine*. Thus, to one of his old friends of the range:

> . . . the older I get the more I think of the old days an the times we had before the bench land granger grabed the grass   there was no law aginst smoking sigeretts then an no need of a whipping post for wife beeters   the fiew men that had wives were so scared of loosing them they generley handeled them mighty tender. the scacity of the females give them considerbal edg those days   I never licked no women but Im shure glad I beet these morilests to the country   its hard to guess what they would have don to me. Chances are Id be making hair bridles now for smoking sigeretts or staying up after twelve oclock.   but they got here to late to hed of my fun an as I am real good now I aint worring much.

Of the offhand watercolor sketches that illustrate and complement the letters, some are as fine as his more studied work. The stories and the letters have another value as well. Being of limited formal schooling, Russell spelled phonetically, and one result is the very sound of cowboy talk in that time and place, the vernacular (minus the profanity) and the drawl, the nonchalant way with grammar, the utter absence of the contrived and "literary." If he had never put a brush to canvas, it is clear in retrospect, he still would have had his niche as an historian of the Old West.

Along toward the mid-1920's, time was running out on him —sciatic rheumatism, a goiter operation, an impaired heart— and he was aware of it. With an old cowpuncher's fatalism and lack of heroics, he took the worst with the best. "Any man that can make a living doing what he likes is lucky, and I'm that. Any time I cash in now, I win," he wrote in 1925. He was by now ahead of the game in another sense, thanks to his businesslike Nancy. His pictures were bringing sums unimaginable in the old days when a ten-dollar sale meant a drink for the house on Charlie and the buyer of the picture was regarded as a sucker. Montanans were proud when the heir to the British throne, who also was a ranch owner north of the Canadian border, bought a Russell painting for an awesome fee. Montanans also believed that if Charlie had lived to hear it, he would have agreed with Con Price when Con said, "I have seen some of Charlie's pictures that he sold for ten dollars at that time, that afterwards he sold to the Prince of Wales for ten thousand dollars that I couldn't see a great deal of difference."

(Indifferent as he was to money, Charlie might have raised a shaggy eyebrow when, after his death, a Montana state legislature committee haggled endlessly over a proposal to purchase for some eighty thousand dollars the Russell pictures that adorned the Mint Saloon. While the committee haggled, the Russell Estate sold them to a New York art gallery for $125,000. The gallery offered the pictures in a group to the Texas millionaire, Amon Carter, who told the gallery to forward the pictures to him without bothering to unpack them. He would immediately send his check for $250,000.)

As twilight was closing in on an October day in 1926, Charlie Russell asked to be driven out into the hills outside Great Falls to look at the sunset. He gazed at it intensely. A few hours later he was dead, at sixty-four. It did not seem possible.

"Try an obituary of him," said Mr. Ferguson the next morning. "If the first three hundred words don't seem right, I'll call it off and we'll bring a prepared one up to date."

I wrote from 8 A.M. until almost noon, and I guess it was all right, because when my father read it in the *Sentinel* that day he said, "In a while, maybe a year, you might be ready for New York."

I knew a surge of pride, and then of dismay. I was in no hurry to go to New York.

Return

On a Sunday in June, 1962, exactly thirty years after I had last seen Montana, the plane that left Newark, New Jersey, in the rainy, humid morning was traveling westward through sunlight almost blinding. All day the country below unrolled like a huge topographical map: Great Lakes, placid Midwestern prairies, the wilder landscape of Western North Dakota, the Missouri River wandering in huge coils, the savage Dakota Montana badlands, the rolling plains of South Central Montana. And then, suddenly, there they were, the Rockies, white-topped and dazzling. I knew a moment of something like panic. What if it were really true that you can't go home again? That time has played too many sad tricks on us all, the living and the dead? . . .

The plane put down at Butte and Helena. A voice from the pilot's quarters announced Missoula in thirty-five minutes. Thirty-five minutes? It had been three and a half hours in the Hupmobile, struggling over Priest Pass and the Continental Divide. (But, then, it had been two whole days and nights from Chicago to Missoula on the old *North Coast Limited*.) The panic was building again as the plane—lumbering a little, it seemed to me—crossed the Divide, slanted down the other side, and soared through Hell Gate Canyon. Was that scar on the south side of Hell Gate, over by the Chicago, Milwaukee and St. Paul tracks, the rockslide that a couple of kids launched on a summer afternoon forty-odd years ago? I wanted to think so.

Now the plane was out of the canyon and flying low over a town that stretched unbelievably out across the prairie. Where the Indians had camped in the spring to dig for camas roots were tree-lined streets and neat homes. What seemed to be a new bridge or two spanned the river. Buildings taller than any I remembered rose above the old ones. But the snow shone on Mount Lolo, eleven miles to the south, and that was right. Snow was always on Lolo. Something else, not immediately to be defined, seemed familiar, as if it were struggling up out of a dream. Then it came to me, and it did indeed have to do with a dream. Just so, in recent years, I had awakened on many a morning having just dreamed of flying west through Hell Gate Canyon into the late afternoon sun, and now it was true. I was home.

I was even more sure of it when, that evening, I strolled around the streets north of the river. There were changes by the score, to be sure. The old Florence Hotel, in whose lobby the traveling salesmen had traded lies and bandied wisecracks straight from glamorous New York City, had been replaced by a new, glossy Florence. A demolition firm was even now at work on the old First National Bank Building where the Human Fly had thrilled his apprehensive public. A loan shop, or something equally unlikely, occupied the premises of the old *Missoulian-Sentinel* office. The alley behind it, a grimy area memorable for the ferocity of fights among restless newsboys waiting for their papers, contained a night club. The new *Missoulian-Sentinel* office on North Higgins Avenue, red brick and plate glass, appeared to be a model plant for a modern small-town newspaper, little as it could ever take its predecessor's place in the heart of a returning son.

It doesn't matter, I said to myself. What mattered was that the sunset still filled the sky with red and bluish lights at nine o'clock and the cool, dry wind moved down the river out of

Hell Gate Canyon, bringing with it the scent of pine. Surely the humid morning in Newark was a year, and not merely a dozen hours, ago. Just as surely, the thirty years since I had last been here were gone in a flash.

To the Florence Hotel the next noon came Ray Rocene, the newspaperman with few peers among the newspapermen I have known. Over a pre-lunch drink we talked as if we were picking up a conversation that had been interrupted only the day before, save for what he told me of the deaths of such friends as French Ferguson and Pat Callahan.

Ray said casually, "You may not have heard that I've more or less retired."

What, I asked, could he mean by that? I had read his characteristically lively "Sports Jabs" column in the *Missoulian* only that morning. Was he saying that he now wrote only one or two columns a week, just to keep his hand in?

"Oh, no," said Ray, entirely seriously. "I still write six a week, but I don't cover the railroads, the Forestry Service and the hotels any more. I've slowed up."

If this, I reflected, was "slowing up," what did his big-city sports-writing counterparts—few of them his equal in sheer talent—do for a living? I thought it best to change the subject in a hurry lest this modest man be embarrassed.

"I don't suppose Kid Jackson is still alive," I said.

Ray smiled.

"A couple of young men around here wish he wasn't, after what happened last week," he said.

The Kid, now seventy-seven, was tending bar in a spot over on Ryman Avenue, Ray continued. Into the saloon one morning had come a pair of brawny truck drivers working on a Federal road-building project. Their language, in the Kid's view, became objectionable. He might not have taken exception to it but for the presence of a woman waking up over an early morning beer at a table in the corner. That the woman was a long-retired West Front Street madam was irrelevant. The Kid had his code. He advised that the young men's vocabulary be toned down. And if it was not, one of them asked, what did the Kid propose to do about it?

"Let us talk about this outside," the Kid suggested.

From a chair near the window, Ray had looked on with interest. The Kid and his two challengers had barely reached the sidewalk when the Kid, pivoting and punching, threw a left hook into the stomach of one of the young men who towered above him, pivoted again, and landed a right hook in the stomach of the other. They fell and were conspicuously ill on the sidewalk. The Kid came back into the bar, winking at Ray and asking, "You know why I didn't go for the chin?"

Ray knew, but pretended not to.

"Didn't want to hurt my hands," said the Kid.

"We'll go around and see him tomorrow," Ray said now. When we arived the next morning the Kid, trim and quick-moving as on the night he had given a boxing lesson to the young man from Spokane almost forty years before, was entertaining his customers at the bar with a running fire of stories. His hands, as he gestured or made a drink, moved with the deftness of his fighting prime. His smile flashed as he saw us come in, and he slid around the end of the bar.

"How long is it you've been away?" he said. "Ten years, fifteen years?"

"Thirty," I said.

"My God," said the Kid, "then it's more than fifty years since I fought Ad Wolgast. . . ."

The morning ran on.

As it long before had seemed to be, time once more was askew: the past and present were one. George Reeves, the lightning telegrapher who represented The Associated Press in a cubicle of the old *Missoulian-Sentinel* office, had aged by no more than ten years during those thirty. Ralph Swartz, in retirement, soft-voiced and cheerful as ever, chatted away through an afternoon that brought back a hundred names and stories. Was there something preservative, I wondered, in the very purity and dryness of this air?

I was sure of it when, a few days later, I drove down the Bitter Root Valley and called upon Bessie K. Monroe, still covering the news there for the *Missoulian* and *Sentinel*, and with the same tireless devotion, as she had been doing through four decades. Mrs. Monroe, looking deceptively like a white-haired grandmother, invited me to accompany her on her rounds of the county courthouse in Hamilton, the town that Marcus Daly created to adjoin his estate there. A certain county official was not in his office.

"Where is he?" Mrs. Monroe demanded of a secretary, "and what is he doing and when will he be back? You might as well tell me, because I'll find out anyhow." The secretary, overwhelmed, told her.

"You are a great woman, B.K.," I said as we walked along to the next office.

"I am a reporter," said Mrs. Monroe calmly.

Time seemed scarcely to have touched these old friends. Was it because, whether still in harness or relaxing, they regarded life as something to be lived and loved rather than as a contest for place and gain? If they still worked, they worked hard. They also went fishing, read books, took a glass of bourbon over talk that ran well into the night, or, like Mrs. Monroe, lingered over a dish of ice cream and went home to write a poem. It was a returning son's first impression that a certain complacency might be read into present-day Montanans' lack of enthusiasm for any and all plans for a more populous, more heavily industrialized State. Upon second thought, it struck me that their detachment made considerable sense. If I were to live here again, it occurred to me, I too would be content to see the nation's fourth largest State retain its country air of not-rich, not-poor, and a population somewhat smaller than that of Cleveland, Ohio.

Let the East come out and spend its vacation money in the

national parks and on dude ranches, the Montanans say; but who would want factory jungles smoking up the high, blue sky from the Dakotas to Idaho? One Butte was enough. Better that the cattle business is finding its way back in small "spreads," that agriculture is being restored by new techniques that heal the wounds of the dry-land farming fiasco.

In politics, I was amused if not surprised to find, Montana was inconsistent as always. The old tradition of grass-roots radicalism having faded, Montana tended to vote Republican and conservative in elections for State and local offices but to send Democrats and liberals to Washington—perhaps, it is said with cheerful irony, to get them out of Montana. If there was a decisive change in the Montana atmosphere, it had been brought about by the withdrawal of The Company—the Anaconda Copper Mining Company—from its old position of open, feudal power. It had sold the newspapers it once controlled to a chain based in the Midwest. It no longer bothered to buy the election of enough members of the State Legislature to protect its interests there, because those interests now were fewer. The artistry of a few legislative lobbyists sufficed. . . .

South from Hamilton and the Bitter Root, over the road that Dougal McCormick and my father and Evan Reynolds and I traveled so long ago on the way to Wisdom and the Harvest Rodeo, I went in a little car half the length of Dougal's long, chocolate-colored Winton. Where the Winton had fiercely fought its way up and across the Continental Divide, the little car drifted along a subtly graded highway and was over the Divide before I realized it. It was almost dismayingly easy. And Wisdom itself, down on the Big Hole Valley floor —it was a different Wisdom. The old one had long since "burned out." The rodeo arena where Ad Jackson had his bad day was gone. So were the boardwalks where cowboys' spurs had rasped. Never mind, there were Bannack and Virginia City off to the south.

Each, when I had last seen it, was all but a ghost town well on the way to decay. Each, some time since then, had been saved from extinction by Montana's increasing awareness of its history, so that Bannack is now a State monument and Virginia City is a breathing likeness of its early-day self. In both, as when I had listened to the stories of the old men on long-gone summer afternoons, I seemed to see Henry Plummer walking catlike toward an incoming stagecoach and asking the passengers, in his even voice, "Anything unusual happen on the road?"—and bad luck for the one who answered with a too detailed description of the highwaymen who had held it up.

Bannack, this afternoon, lay in utter stillness, birds winging in and out of Cy Skinner's windowless saloon where the Plummer gang once roistered. Mice scampered across the dirt floor of the log cabin jail where Sheriff Plummer chained desperadoes to await execution on the gallows where he himself was to die. By contrast Virginia City—seventy-five miles away—hummed on the evening of this day. The hum was of tourist traffic, visiting parents and children walking from one reconstructed store front to another along Wallace Street, a mechanical piano blaring old tunes in the Bale of Hay Saloon, youngsters staring in awe at the old stagecoach that stands before the Wells, Fargo office as naturally as if the horses had just been unhitched and led away to be curried, fed and watered. From Boot Hill, as the dusk came down, strolled travelers who had been gazing with another kind of awe at the graves of the terrible Boone Helm and the four who were hanged with him on that January day in '64.

To one who had always been chary of the archness of "restored" historical places, it was clear that the clock had been correctly turned back here. This, I said to myself, must be Virginia City as it was, and retired contentedly to my quarters in the spruce little hotel named for old Bill Fairweather, head of the discovery party that struck it richer than a man dared dream, just up the gulch where the alders grow. And I fancied, as I dropped off to sleep, that I could hear little Mollie Sheehan skipping across Daylight Gulch, playing hookey from the schoolroom where the preoccupied Professor Thomas J. Dimsdale was writing his *Vigilantes of Montana*. . . .

The little car took me north the next day, over the Continental Divide by the Pipestone Pass, and on into Butte. Only a little reflection should have told me that, The Company having closed down its major mining operations, this could not be the roaring place it had once been. Still, I was unprepared for the air of desolation that hung over it. Early on a mid-week afternoon the streets were strangely quiet. Miners' metal hats were glumly stacked in secondhand store windows, and that in itself was a telltale sign; when a miner parts with his metal hat, he has left for good. Old men with bitter faces and accident-maimed bodies stood on the corners or dozed over their beer in the bars. Above the city, up there on The Richest Hill on Earth, in whose deep shafts Heinze's and Daly's miners had fought one another to the death, the only apparent activity was taking place in the vicinity of an ugly, open pit mine. Where the Atlantic Bar had stood, home of the green-felted craps games and the blackjack dealers, there was now a soda fountain. A small, dark cloud of despair, no larger than a blackjack dealer's agile hand, hovered on the returning son's horizon.

I dropped into a saloon and inquired of a bartender what mistaken notion of progress had overcome this once turbulent camp.

"The God-damned reformers," he snarled. "The politicians. There was a time a man could come over here from Missoula or Helena, ready to drop fifty dollars or a hundred but have a little fun just the same, and everybody was better off for it. Nobody dragged him kicking and screaming into the Atlantic or the Rialto for a go at the wheel. But somebody decided they'd rather have reform and a dead place."

I went back to my motel to while away what remained of the afternoon and to wait for the evening. After dark, surely, Butte would be something like its old self. I would have a good Italian dinner at one of those restaurants in Meaderville, one course after another, with the good red table wine keeping pace with them.

"You won't find one of those restaurants," said the motel proprietor. "You won't find anything left of Meaderville."

He was right. Nor was Butte by night any improvement on Butte by day. It was, if anything, even more somber. On Galena and Mercury Streets, where pennies had tapped on windows and soiled but fetching doves had spoken invitingly, was the blankness of warehouses and garages. Where now was the Butte of Stanley Ketchel, the murderous middleweight, and "Fat Jack" Jones, the cadaverous hack driver, the Butte of Marcus Daly and William Andrews Clark? Even Clark's three-story, red brick, dormer-windowed mansion at Granite and Idaho Streets, once Butte's and the copper king's pride, was peeling and seedy.

It was time to get away from this semi-ghost town, and I did, as early as possible the next morning, bound for Helena. My father's city would not fail me, and it did not.

The air was crystalline as always, the twilight violet, the sunrise sudden and brilliant. The weather-beaten mansions of the pioneer merchants and bankers seemed not a day older. Montana's two metropolises, Great Falls and Billings, bustled with enterprise. Helena retained the muted charm of the town through whose streets my father and I had strolled some forty years ago. Well, yes, here too there were some changes. A motor-drawn tourist train, "The Last Chancer," tootled about those streets several times daily, stopping at historic sites. At the head of the Gulch an artists' colony now occupied the quarters once inhabited by ladies practicing another art. The State Historical Society had acquired a handsome new building of its own, to the good fortune of all students of the Old West. Planes droned across the sky and circled down to land at the airport in the Valley of the Prickly Pear. The Helena *Independent*, like the *Missoulian*, had moved to new and shinier quarters. Still, I could enjoy the illusion that I had last been here not more than a week before.

Walking up Edwards Street, I stopped to gaze at the little house perched on the side of Last Chance Gulch where young Martin Hutchens took lodgings on that November day he arrived here in 1889. I seemed again to hear him say, "We used to call it the Queen City of the Rockies . . ." and as his voice came back to me I saw Tommy Cruse riding down the Gulch on his great day in the Panic of '93, and Federal Marshal X. Beidler talking the hours away with other old-timers, and the courtly Colonel Wilbur Fisk Sanders stepping into the Montana Club designed by Cass Gilbert, destroyed by fire and rebuilt according to the great architect's original plans. It came to me suddenly that my father's town was now my town as well, along with my other town, Missoula, just as his Montana had been my Montana for as long as I could remember.

There was a plane I had to take soon for the East and the workaday world, but I would come back whenever I could, because Montana is where I belong, in place and time—the place that is like no other, the time that is not simply time, but past and present intermingling like those colors in a mountain sunset.